WALKING WITH GOD

BETH D. JONES

Walking with God

Published by Spiritually Fit Publications
www.SpirituallyFit.org

Refreshing Waters Ministries
P. O. Box 452
Butler, MO 64730
(660) 227-9217
Email: elizabethdjones@gmail.com

Published in the United States of America

ISBN: 0-9722592-9-5

$10.99

Dedication and Thanks

Dedicated to my Lord and Best Friend Jesus Christ. To whom belongs the glory and the honor and the praise, forever and ever. I love you, sweet Jesus. Thank You for all You've done for me. May this work bring you glory.

A special thanks to my husband Ray Jones, who has always believed in me. Ray, you are the most intelligent, funniest, interesting man I know. Thank you for always encouraging me to go for my dreams and that the sky is the limit. I love you. For our daughter Heather, you are my special gift from God. You are not only my daughter, but my precious friend. I love you so much. Thank you for all your prayers and encouragement to me that I can see my dreams come true. You and Kyle have given me such great joy through our grandchildren, Annabelle and Violet. Our daughter Eden, you are my refiner's fire in life. God has used you to teach me much about Jesus' unconditional love. I love you, and you and Logan have blessed me so much with another adorable grandchild, Jacob. Our youngest daughter Leah, your life has made an incredible imprint upon my life. Your birth brought great joy to my life. I love you with all my heart. My one and only sister Maria, what would I ever do without you, my dear, precious friend? Thank you for always loving me no matter what, and encouraging me to press on and to keep my eyes on Jesus. Writer, speaker, excellent wife and home-schooling mom, Cindy Rushton, you are my role model for true godly success. Thank you for all you've imparted into my life, and helping me to reach for my dreams. This is the year! Kim Weber, you are forever my inspiration as the Proverbs 31 woman. And we share a deep love for chocolate. Gala Palmgren, you are a woman of God, whose life has deeply impacted me and blessed me. I love your writing and your beautiful heart. You are a rare diamond. Suzy Bunton, you've inspired me to speak God's words. Thanks for all the encouragement, prayers and laughs. Lawrence and Louise Wilson, Crystal Tinsley, Doris Goddard, Brenda Wilson, Betty Spangler, Frances Lawrence and so many others who prayed so long for Leah, may God bless you 100-fold. Marcheta DeVries and Terrie Ramsey, you are women of wisdom, discernment and encouragement. Thank you for keeping me and my family covered in prayer, and believing in me. Debbie Nagel, thank you for always being there for our family through the years. You are my sis! Diane Bishop, you've imparted so much into my life and have been an excellent teacher. You are a woman of God, and you walk your talk. Ruth Christian, your very presence calms and encourages me. I can't wait to go to Africa with you. Heather Hamilton, thank you for seeing greatness in me, and for always making me laugh. "Beth, stop being so serious!" LOL. I love you, girlfriend! For all the writers, speakers, bloggers who have inspired and encouraged me to write this book and to blog, and to be all that God desires me to be, thank you with all my heart. To my English teacher in high school, whose eyebrow raised when she read my writing and she encouraged me that I was a good writer, thank you. To my counselor of many years and friend Darrell, thank you with everything inside me for telling me that my past would not dictate my future, and God had a great plan for my life. To Al Ridge, who envisioned things for me that I could not even imagine, I miss you and I'm glad you can walk now—up in heaven with Jesus. To his wife Vicki Ridge, who prayed so many times for me and saw my potential. To my parents, who taught me a strong work ethic, thank you, and daddy, I love you. To all those family and friends who have prayed for our family throughout our difficult years, thanks are simply not enough. Keep praying! I love you all. For those who edited this book, Ruby, Ray, Heather, and Maria, may the Lord bless you for your unselfish time, wise advice, and constructive criticism to make this a much better book. Iron sharpens iron. God knew the perfect timing. To all writers, speakers, and bloggers, everywhere, thank you for inspiring me with good books. "Fill your paper with the breathings of your heart." - William Wordsworth

Table of Contents

Introduction

For those of you who already pray, at first glance this book might seem, as Sherlock Holmes would say, "Elementary, my dear Watson!" We believers know that we need to pray, and that we need to pray more. But why should we pray? First, we should pray because Jesus prayed. He is our example. "Now it came to pass in those days that He went to the mountains to pray, and continued all night in prayer to God."[1] If Jesus the Son of God prayed, how much more do we need to do it! Second, the Bible commands us to pray. "Pray without ceasing."[2] We pray because we want to obey God's word. It is our Christian duty to pray. Simply put, it is the right and good thing to do. Third, we pray because we need God. The Syro-Phoenician woman realized that only Jesus could set her

---

[1] Luke 6:17, New King James Version Bible.
[2] 1 Thessalonians 5:17, NKJV Bible.

demonized daughter free. Her response to Jesus calling her a dog, the Jews' derogatory name for Gentiles, was that even the little dogs eat the children's crumbs under the table. Jesus commended her for her faith and delivered her daughter.[3] Fourth, we should pray because there is joy in spending time with God. For me, there's nothing like putting on a worship CD and coming into the presence of the Lord. It's refreshing and uplifting. My spirit is strengthened, and then I can go on to face the challenges of daily life after spending time with God.

These are all very good reasons to pray. However, I want to encourage you with a fresh reason or praying. Pray because God wants to just be with you and me! God loves to spend time with us. He delights in His creation. The Song of Solomon says, "Let me see your face, Let me hear your voice; For your voice is sweet, and your face is lovely."[4] God wants to walk and talk with us each day just as He did with Enoch. "Enoch lived sixty-five years, and begot Methuselah. After he begot Methuselah, Enoch walked with God three hundred years, and had sons and daughters. And Enoch walked with God; and he was not, for God took him."[5] Enoch walked with God three hundred years, every day—talking to Him, listening to Him, spending time with Him and just hanging out with

[3] Mark 7:24-30, NKJV Bible.
[4] Song of Solomon 2:14, NKJV Bible.
[5] Genesis 5:21-24, NKJV Bible.

God. Then Enoch just disappeared—he walked right into heaven one day with God, without every dying! This is what God wants to do with you and me. He wants to talk with us, as He did with Adam in the garden.[6]

Intimacy with God is my heart's passion. My desire is to impart that fire to our children, our grandchildren, and to other believers. This book has been written to encourage God's people to seek His face, to develop deeper intimacy with Him in prayer and in His word each day. I believe this is a timely word from the Lord for the Church. The Church at large still does not realize that our strength comes from prayer. Intimacy with the Father. Walking with God, as Enoch did. Sitting at Jesus' feet like Mary of Bethany did.

There is an expression well known in churches: PUSH. Pray Until Something Happens. PUSH. For example, the woman with the issue of blood pushed through the crowds, pushed through her fear, pushed through all the obstacles to receive her healing from Jesus.[7] The little, old widow pestered the judge until He gave her what she asked for of him.[8] A sinful woman broke the alabaster jar and poured

---

[6] Genesis 2:7-25, NKJV Bible.
[7] Luke 8:40-48.
[8] Luke 18:1-8.

the fragrant perfume over Jesus' feet. [9] Adoration. Prayer. Worship.

Blind Bartamaeus cried out in desperation for a touch from God.[10] David prayed, running for his life, hiding in a cave.[11] Hannah prayed for a male child, her heart's deepest desire because she was barren.[12] Esther fasted and petitioned God to save her life and her people's lives from destruction.[13] Jesus prayed in the garden of Gethsemane: "My Father, if it is possible, don't make me suffer by having me drink from this cup. But do what you want, and not what I want."[14]

Prayer draws us near to God. As we come into His presence, He speaks to us about how much He loves us. We receive a revelation of His mercy and forgiveness toward us. His Holy Spirit also convicts us of sin, and leads us to repentance, changing our hearts. "I will give you a new heart and put a new spirit within you; I will take the heart of stone out of your flesh and give you a heart of flesh."[15] As God gives us greater revelation about His love and grace in the prayer closet, it transforms us "from glory to glory" into the image of Christ.[16] We then take that

---

[9] Luke 7:37-38.
[10] Mark 10:47.
[11] I Samuel 24:1-7.
[12] 1 Samuel 1:10-11.
[13] Esther 4:13-17.
[14] Matthew 26:39, Contemporary English Version Bible.
[15] Ezekiel 36:26, NKJV.
[16] 2 Corinthians 3:18, NKJV.

glory to a lost and dying world, sharing His love and grace with them. God's word says, "Be still and know that I am God."[17] Be still. Be quiet, and listen to His voice. God will speak to you. Just come away and be with Him, and pray. Let His love wash over you and refresh you like the rain. Discover the depths of His love for you. "Launch out into the deep," Jesus told Peter.[18] Dive deeper into intimacy with God. Pray. It's even better than chocolate. To be in the presence of God is beyond anything you can even imagine. God just wants to be with us! "Deep calls unto deep at the noise of Your waterfalls."[19] Go deeper with God. Deeper in intimacy with God. Go ahead, step in…the water feels so good!

---

[17] Psalm 46:10, NKJV.
[18] Luke 5:4, NKJV.
[19] Psalm 42:7, NKJV.

Chapter 1
Walking With God

Prayer is simply friendship with God. It is talking with God and Him talking with us, while we avail our hearts to listen to Him. God has a still, small voice, but I've also known Him to be rather loud and insistent at times! My desire is to walk with God as Enoch did, until I am no more.[20] Prayer is intimacy with the Lord. We get a picture of the deep intimacy prayer can be in the passage of John 13:22-25. John was the disciple who laid his head on Jesus' breast. He could hear the Lord's heartbeat. Our ultimate goal is to hear our Father's heartbeat as well—we need to know His desires, His thoughts, and His ways. The Bible says, "For it is time to seek the Lord, Till He comes and rains righteousness on you."[21] The Bible says to draw near

---

[20] Genesis 5:24, NKJV Bible.
[21] Hosea 10:12, NKJV Bible.

to God, and He will draw near to us.[22] We can't draw near to God if we don't pray. Many times people are afraid to come into the presence of the Lord because of their sins. They are under condemnation. They are ashamed. But God is the only one we can go to with our sins. He is the only one who can save us from them. The Bible says Jesus became the propitiation for our sins.[23] Christ became the substitute on the cross for our sins. He died there instead of us. Our sins deserve the wrath and punishment of the Lord. Jesus became our mediator, willingly laying down His life, so that He could take our place. He took the chastisement for our peace. (Isaiah 53:5) Because of Jesus' redemptive work on the cross, our sins are forgiven.

When we receive Him as Lord and Savior, all our sins— past, present, and future are forgiven. And, we become forever sealed by the Holy Spirit, the "earnest" or "deposit," the guarantee of our inheritance in Christ.[24] So we don't have to be afraid to come into God's presence. He loves us. He longs to forgive us, restore us, and heal us. He will not turn us away, but will embrace us as the father did the prodigal son.[25] We soon will spend eternity with God the Father. He will wipe away every tear, and there will be no more pain, no more sorrow—only unspeakable

---

[22] James 4:8, NKJV Bible.
[23] 1 John 2:2, NKJV Bible.
[24] Ephesians 1:7-14, NKJV Bible.
[25] Luke 15:11-32, NKJV Bible.

joy in His presence, forever and ever. (Revelation 21:4; 1 Peter 1:8)

Prayer is simply enjoying God now. Think of having a cup of coffee or a cold drink with a good friend. You are relaxed and are having fun. You talk easily, naturally. You laugh, you cry, you share each other's sorrows. You know, understand, and love each other. That is the way it is in friendship with God. He wants us to pour out our hearts to Him. (Psalm 62:8) He also wants to share His thoughts, even His secrets, with us. (Daniel 2:28) So prayer is like going out for a cup of cappuccino or a refreshing drink with God. The point is to cultivate intimacy with our Heavenly Father. He is readily available to us, every day, any time. He never goes on vacation, He doesn't have call waiting, and He doesn't have to try to squeeze you in somewhere, between appointments on His daily planner. Now pour yourself a good, strong cup of coffee, and settle down comfortably in your favorite nook for a heart-to-heart with Jesus. There is no friend like Him. He's just waiting to talk to you right now.

Chapter Two
The Invitation

"The beginning is the most important part of the work." ~ Plato

God has given us an invitation to come into His presence through prayer. He wants to spend time with us, just as we enjoy spending time with our loved ones. Prayer is called "the secret place" in Psalm 91:1-2. "He who dwells in the secret place of the most high shall abide under the shadow of the Almighty. I will say of the LORD, "He is my refuge and my fortress; my God, in Him I will trust." Here in the secret place God will speak to you about His great love for you. He invites you to put aside all your worries and concerns, and just rest in his presence. If you are struggling with sins, He will take those, too. Jesus bore them at the cross for you so you would be forgiven. God just wants to be with you! He's crazy about you!

In the Garden of Eden, Adam and Eve had just sinned, doing exactly what God had told them not to do, and causing future generations to suffer the consequences of that one disobedient act. Yet, God walked through the garden, looking for them, and asking Adam, "Where are you?"[26]

The passage is heartbreaking. And, regardless of his mistake, Adam knew how much God loved him and wanted to be with him. God is also looking for you as well—He wants to know where you are. He desires to spend time with you, to let you know how deeply he loves you. Many times our daily lives are so busy, we often just hastily pray as we get ready for the day. We say a routine blessing at mealtimes, and ask God to forgive us of our sins. Yes, our sins, as we're lying down exhausted in bed at night after making another hectic to-do list for the next day. Yet, God has given us an invitation to come away with Him, and be with Him: "Get up, my darling. Let's go away, my beautiful one."[27] The unabashed love story of King Solomon and the Shulamite woman has been explained by some Biblical scholars as symbolic. I believe it shows the fiery passion God has for His people—Jesus' love song to His Bride, the Church.

---

[26] Genesis 3:7-10, NKJV Bible.
[27] Song of Solomon 2:13, New Century Version Bible.

In this wonderful romance, Solomon (the Beloved) is wooing the Shulamite, describing the effect she has upon Him and how much He desires to be with her. He is smitten with her love. For Him there is no other love. He just wants to be with her and He is calling her. Jesus is eager to find His Bride, to be with her. God cannot wait to hear her speak to Him. "Show me your face, and let Me hear your voice. Your voice is sweet, and your face is lovely." (Song of Solomon 2:14) This poetic book characterizes the heart of the Father, how He longs to spend time with His masterpiece! As Stasi Eldredge describes eloquently in her book, *Captivating*, we are the glory of God: "Creation in its early stages begins like any great work of art – with uncut stone or a mass of clay, a rough sketch, a blank sheet of music...Then God begins to fashion the raw materials he has made, like an artist working with the stone or sketch or page before him...It is more astonishing than we could possibly imagine..The greatest of all masterpieces is emerging...God sets His own image on the earth. He creates a being like himself...Nothing in creation even comes close. Picture Michelangelo's *David*. He is magnificent. And yet, the Master says that something is not good, not right. Something is missing and that something is Eve. She is the crescendo, the final, astonishing work of God. Woman.

She is the Master's finishing touch."[28] We were made in the image of God. We were created for *intimacy*. Too often it's easy to get into a daily routine, forgetting the most important thing—our relationship with God. When Martha expressed frustration to Jesus about her sister not helping her get things ready, Jesus did not rebuke Martha for working in the kitchen; after all, she was doing a great thing, making dinner for God! Jesus reproached her, however, for not prioritizing. "The Master said, "Martha, dear Martha, you're fussing far too much and getting yourself worked up over nothing. One thing only is essential, and Mary has chosen it—it's the main course, and won't be taken from her."[29]

Just one thing is necessary: time with God. It is vital that we set aside time each day to be with Him. This quiet time will vary from person to person. Though Larry Lea's Series, *Will You Not Tarry One Hour* motivated many believers in the 1970's to spend at least an hour a day in prayer, your quiet time may consist of only ten to fifteen minutes in the car commuting to work! As long as you set aside a portion of your day to sit at the feet of Jesus—silent before Him, being refreshed, renewed, lingering in His Holy Presence, perhaps meditating on a Psalm or a Proverb, or listening to a praise or worship tape, this is all

---

28 *Captivating*, John and Stasi Eldredge, Nelson Books, Nashville, TN, 2005, pp. 23-25.
29 Luke 10:38-42, The Message Bible.

that matters. By prioritizing your day, you are responding to God's invitation of intimacy.

This time with God is our necessary Bread, the Manna from heaven that sustains us daily. We can't do anything without Jesus. "I am the vine, and you are the branches. He who abides in me, and I in Him, bears much fruit; for without Me they can do nothing." [30] Many people come under condemnation because of a neglected prayer life. Too often they look at spiritual giants such as Pastor Cho, the leader of the largest church in Korea. God has not led everyone to pray three hours a day! He just wants a willing heart. Five minutes of sincere prayer is better than I-have-to-pray religious duty. "For a day in your courts is better than a thousand elsewhere."[31] God just wants to *be* with you and me! He is thrilled with five minutes of time with you, just as I am so happy when our grown, married daughter Heather calls to say hello and chats for only a couple of minutes! It's your heart that God wants.

Plato said the beginning is the most important part of the work. Take the first step. Start with a couple of minutes of prayer at a set time each day. A good time to start is the early morning, when you first wake up. Devote the day to God. Ask His Holy Spirit to lead your prayer. Tell Him that you want to hear His voice. "My sheep hear My

---

[30] John 15:5, NKJV Bible.
[31] Psalm 84:10, English Standard Bible.

voice."[32]   As you faithfully begin to meet with God each day, your hunger for His presence will begin to grow.   Of course, the truth is that sometimes when we pray, the time is not always that exciting!   We may often feel distracted or even bored!

As Michal Ann Goll says in *A Call To The Secret Place*, we need to ask God to help us to pray.   "We need help to prevent our minds from wandering.   If you've ever tried to spend time alone with the Lord, you know what I mean.   You seek quiet and a break – but the minute you sit down "the list" takes over your mind.   You think, *I can't sit here. There's wet laundry in the dryer, and I've got to pay this bill, and...and....and...*You realize you're not getting anywhere spiritually, and you give up."[33] Don't give up.   Don't give in to the enemy who hates prayer!   "And Satan trembles when he sees the weakest saint upon his knees."[34] A few minutes each day of heartfelt prayer can make an incredible difference in your life and in the lives of those around you!

Dr. Richard Swenson, M.D., writes in his book *Margin* that being hurried is the norm in today's society.   This is an unprecedented age, in which progress, problems, stress, and overload have crowded out all the margin in our lives

---

[32] John 10:27, NKJV Bible.

[33] *A Call To The Secret Place*, Michal Anne and Jim Goll, Destiny Image Publishers, March 31, 2003, p. 21.

[34] *Great Thoughts & Funny Sayings*, William Cowper,Tyndale House Publishers, March 1, 1993, p. 251

for right relationships, which are vital for our well-being.[35] Not only must we manage our stress today, but we must reduce it as well. We can do ourselves a big favor by slowing down: seeking simplicity, balance, and rest.[36] We find all these three things when we take time out to pray. "Come to Me, all you who labor and are heavy laden and overburdened, and I will cause you to rest, [I will ease and relieve and refresh your souls.] Take my yoke upon you and learn of Me, for I am gentle (meek) and humble (lowly) in heart, and you will find rest (relief and ease and refreshment and recreation and blessed quiet) for your souls. For my yoke is wholesome (useful, good-not harsh, hard, sharp, or pressing, but comfortable, gracious and pleasant), and My burden is light and easy to be borne."[37]

Just as God our Creator rested on the seventh day, so we His created must take sabbaticals—weekly, and even daily times of refreshing and restoration for our souls. Life demands so much of us. Our spouses, our children, or our jobs can drain our emotional energy. Spiritually, we are in a war each day with the world, the flesh, and the devil. Seeking out time with God, allowing His Spirit to search our hearts, will renew us, and give us strength. "In returning and rest you shall be saved; In quietness and

---

[35] *Margin*, Dr. Richard Swenson, M.D., Nav Press, December 13, 1999, pp. 35-36.
[36] Ibid, p. 185.
[37] Matthew 11:28-30, Amplified Bible.

confidence shall be your strength."[38] Sometimes when I am so busy throughout the day, homeschooling our daughter, running errands, and cleaning the house, I feel exhausted by dinnertime at 5 p.m. Stress, fatigue, and hunger seem to be my trigger points for getting frustrated, and my meltdown usually occurs right about the time my family is making demands for supper and my attention.

When I'm running on empty, the only thing I have to give is a piece of my mind! I have found that if I just take a few minutes alone with God and pray, He gives me that "second wind" to keep going. His presence fills me back up, and gives me the strength and stamina that I need for the rest of day. Sometimes we also need to just stop what we're doing in the middle of our busy lives, and focus on God. One afternoon I had a lot to do around the house. It was one of those days when it seemed nothing was getting accomplished, despite my frantic and frustrated efforts. Our daughter Leah, at that time ten years old, called my name several times from the den. I was folding clothes, while wondering how I was going to prepare dinner that night. I called out to her, "Not now, Leah!" But her sweet, little voice was insistent crying out, "Mom, come here! I want to show you something!"

A little annoyed, but curious, I figured she had drawn another pretty picture of a horse to proudly display. I went into the den, as she stood by the window, intently looking

---

[38] Isaiah 30:15, NKJV Bible.

out at the backyard. It must be a stray dog or cat, I mused. I went over to her and impatiently said, "Well, what is it?" "Look at the sunset!" she said, pointing to the sky. I looked, and the sky was painted with incredible orange and pink, bold strokes, something only our God could do! "Isn't it pretty, mom?" she said. I smiled at her, tears of conviction and gratitude in my eyes. "Yes, it's beautiful. Isn't God great to make a sunset like that?" I replied. "I knew you would like it," she said, smiling and admiring God's breath-taking art with me.

Don't miss the beautiful sunsets. Take time out to appreciate and enjoy God's handiwork in nature, to behold the beauty of the Lord—His awesome, majestic presence. Look up at the stars with your husband or wife. Watch a red cardinal with your child. Plant some bright, yellow tulips in your yard. Go for a walk with your family, and admire the squirrels, the dragonflies, the bunny rabbits. Enjoy God's magnificent creation, and praise Him!

Look all around you at this beautiful earth He has made for you and me. Talk to Him as you are walking in the woods, or sitting in the sun at the park, feeling the wind on your cheeks, and watching the geese. Go into your bedroom, and pour out your heart before the Lord—cry, laugh, or be silent and just listen. He wants to speak to you great and mighty things.[39] God desires to just hold you and

---

[39] Jeremiah 33:3, NKJV Bible.

tell you how much He loves you. He has given you an invitation to come into His presence, to be intimate with you, just as He walked and talked with Adam and Eve in the garden. He invites you to come away with Him, as the Beloved did the Shulamite woman, so He can see your face and hear your voice. He wants you to bring all your daily cares and concerns to Him, and for you to just rest in His arms of love. You have a few minutes right now. The door is wide open.

Chapter Three

"But I Don't Hear God's Voice"

A few times I have been approached by people and asked, "How do I hear the voice of God?" A couple of times people have asked me to pray to hear God's voice for them, because they said they couldn't hear His voice. I quickly told them to seek God for themselves! Every believer can hear God's voice. Jesus said, "My sheep hear My voice."[40] Why is it then that many Christians say they have trouble hearing, or at least recognizing, God's voice?

There are two primary reasons we can't hear God's voice: (1) Sin prevents us from hearing God's voice, and (2) we don't recognize God's voice when He does speak. First, let's look at the Creation story in Genesis. God created male and female in His very image. Dutch Sheets

---

[40] John 10:27, NKJV Bible.

writes in *Intercessory Prayer*, that when Adam walked on earth, all of God's creation did a double-take. For a moment they thought they were seeing God![41] Adam was made in the exact likeness of God's Spirit—mirroring God's very essence, he was God's crowning glory. Adam and Eve were in the Garden of Eden, walking and talking with God, face to face! Just imagine. Taking a walk with God. Talking with Him. Just like you and me might walk in the woods with our spouse, or a close friend. Looking at the beautiful birds. Laughing at a brown-eyed squirrel, with his cheeks full of nuts. Looking at a gorgeous sunset. Adam and Eve did this in Eden. They talked with God, just as they spoke with each other. There were no walls of unforgiveness, fear, or distrust. Just open, honest, intimate communication, flowing freely between them all. I wonder what God's voice sounds like? Revelation 1:15 says His voice is like the sound of many waters.

About a year ago, our family flew to New York to see Niagara Falls, one of my dreams come true. I love waterfalls. The sound of the falls is so powerful, it is almost deafening. The waterfalls are breathtakingly beautiful; it is magnificent to see and to hear. I imagine that God's voice must be like this—loud, powerful and compelling; yet, so kind, loving and good.

When sin entered the picture in the Garden of Eden, then Adam and Eve were cast out by God. Adam now

---

[41] *Intercessory Prayer*, Dutch Sheets, Regal Books, p. 26.

would have to work all the days of his life. Eve would desire her husband's authority. Their lives became marked with sorrow as their son Cain killed his brother son Abel out of jealousy, and wickedness grew quickly upon the earth. Sin keeps us from clearly hearing God's voice, and it ultimately leads to death. Finally, the Lord was sorry He had made man, because man had become so evil.[42] He sent a world-wide flood to destroy all but a remnant who found favor in His sight. Noah, the only one on earth who could clearly hear the voice of the Lord! Others laughed at him and mocked him. Sure, sure, there was going to be so much water falling from the sky that it would kill everyone!

Their hearts had become so hardened with sin, they could not even hear the Lord's sure warnings. Sin had made them unable to hear God's voice! Sometimes we are not able to hear God's voice because of sin in our lives. Sin puts a barrier between us and God. But there is good news! When we come to the cross and repent, that barrier is removed. Sin is not always the reason we have trouble distinguishing God's voice. Many times, believers hear God's voice, but don't recognize it; especially, when they have a sudden impression or urge to take groceries to a needy family in church or to speak to a stranger. Could it be the Voice of God? It very well may be; actually, it may be God's voice directing us to His purpose! All too often,

---

[42] Genesis 6:6, NKJV Bible.

we miss our blessings or the ability to bless others because we have a false expectation of what God's voice sound like. The Bible tells that His is a still, small voice.[43] His voice sometimes is a faint impression, even something unplanned, such as, *Call your uncle. He needs to talk to someone.* You might think, *I haven't talked to him in years!* But it's God.

The Lord may move you to do something kind for a stranger: "Remember to welcome strangers, because some who have done this have welcomed angels without knowing it."[44] God's voice might even sound like your own voice: *I should apologize to my co-worker. She didn't deserve that sarcastic remark.* This is the voice of the Holy Spirit convicting you. God will never violate His own word. Anything we hear in our hearts that contradicts Scripture is not of God! We also know from the Bible that God is love.[45] Any voice that we hear that is not motivated by love is not God's voice. Would God say something condemning or judgmental to someone? Would God tell anyone she is a failure or her life has no purpose? No. God's word says, "For I know the thoughts that I think toward you, says the Lord, thoughts of peace and not of evil, to give you a future and a hope."[46] The Bible also says, "Now we hope for the blessings God has for his children.

---

[43] 1 Kings 19:12, NKJV Bible.
[44] Hebrews 13:2, New Century Version Bible.
[45] 1 John 4:8, NKJV Bible.
[46] Jeremiah 29:11, NKJV Bible.

These blessings, which cannot be destroyed or be spoiled or lose their beauty, are kept in heaven for you."[47]

God has good things in store for us. Jeremiah 29:11 says that God has a future and a hope for us. In fact, He has saved the best for last![48] God is always speaking to His people to let them know how much He loves them and has great plans for them, but we are not always listening. Sometimes we don't or can't hear His voice. The first requirement for hearing God's voice is that you are saved. If you are not, please stop right here and pray to receive Jesus Christ as your Lord and Savior. He is the best thing that ever happen to me! Jesus is my Best Friend. He wants to be yours, too. He wants to bless you, to take care of you, and to spend eternity with you. God loves you so much!

The Bible says in Acts 2:38 that all who repent and ask Jesus Christ for the forgiveness of sins will be saved, and will receive the gift of the Holy Spirit. You will spend forever with God in heaven! It will be better than anything we can even imagine! The second requirement to hearing God's voice is that you pray. Go to the source Himself. Pray, ask God to hear His voice, and for Him to block out any other voices! Be hungry for God, and He will fill you with good things.[49] Read God's word. Study it and

---

[47] 1 Peter 1:4, New Century Version Bible.
[48] 1 Corinthians 2:9, NKJV Bible.
[49] Luke 9:13-17, NKJV Bible.

meditate on it. God penned these words to us through His scribes. The Bible is the very mind of God. It tells us what He thinks, how He feels. It contains great wisdom that God desires to give to His people.[50] It warns us of hard times to come. (Revelation 1, Revelation 13:1-18.) It is our instruction manual for life (Psalm 119:105; Proverbs 2, Proverbs 3.) Most of all, it is God's love story written just for us. Jesus has inscribed us on the palms of His hands.[51] The third requirement to hearing God's voice is that you steer clear of sin. If there is known sin in your life, this will keep you from correctly discerning God's voice. Get rid of the sin, because you are a new creation now.[52] God has called you to be holy.[53] Repent and receive His forgiveness. Sin affects our ability to hear from God. Develop a teachable, repentant heart. If you are a new believer, it takes time to discern God's voice. It is that same gentle voice who prompted you to come to the front of the church, to respond at the Christian concert's altar call or in your car driving at night. The same quiet voice that tells you to love your children and have patience with them, or to encourage your husband's heart. As you attend church each week, read your Bible, and pray, you will gain confidence about knowing God's voice.

---

[50] 2 Timothy 3:15, NKJV Bible.
[51] Isaiah 49:16, NKJV Bible.
[52] Colossians 3:5-10, NKJV Bible.
[53] Colossians 3:12, NKJV Bible.

Satan is a master at disguise; he may try to imitate God's voice, but the spirit behind it is not one of unconditional love. He might even try to trick you into doing good things: *Give that beggar on the street corner your rent money!* Yes, God might want you to give away your rent money as an act of faith. Sometimes God will tell us to do things that make absolutely no sense in the natural! It requires faith. But it is accompanied by supernatural peace, an inner knowing and witness to your spirit.[54] Joyce Meyer says let peace be your umpire. If you are feeling worry, confusion, unrest, or fear inside about a decision, you can be sure that it is not the voice of God directing you! God's voice gives you peace! Satan's job is to kill, steal, and destroy (John 10:10.) He is using the same old line that he used on Eve. "Did God really say that you must not eat fruit from any tree in the garden?"[55]

The enemy wants to deceive and to confuse you. Our greatest weapon against him is God's word. This is the weapon Jesus used when he was led into the wilderness to be tempted by the devil. In all three temptations that Satan used to fight Him, Jesus responded with, "It is written in the Scriptures."[56] We won't be able to use this weapon of warfare unless we know what the Bible says. That is why it

---

[54] Philippians 4:7, NKJV Bible.
[55] Genesis 3:1, New Century Version Bible.
[56] Luke 4, New Century Version Bible.

is important to spend time every day reading and studying the Bible and praying. Satan will do all he can to try to keep you from praying and reading the Bible each day. In addition to prayer, fasting also sharpens our spiritual ears to hear God's voice. Jesus talked about the importance of fasting to his disciples. He said "When you fast," not "If you fast."[57]

Jesus is the embodiment of all we should be, and he fasted and prayed.[58] If you are not used to fasting, it is hard at first. Personally, I have never found fasting to be easy! But it has become easier over the years as I have learned to crucify my flesh daily. You may start out fasting just one meal, then build up to longer periods without food. A few days of fasting is not dangerous to your health, unless you have special health concerns such as diabetes, heart problems, or other medical conditions. In this case, seek your physician's advice before fasting. For those who are healthy, fasting actually benefits you physically. It rids your body of toxins. Initially, you might experience temporary discomfort such as severe hunger, anxiety, impatience, or irritability. On the second day, physical discomforts are common such as weakness, dizziness, tiredness, hunger pains, and headaches from sugar or caffeine withdrawal.[59] The first three days are usually the hardest, but you will

---

[57] Matthew 6:16-18, NKJV Bible.
[58] Matthew 4:1-2, NKJV Bible.
[59] *7 Basic Steps to Successful Fasting and Praying*, Bill Bright, New Life Publications, Orlando, FL, 1995, p. 7.

begin feeling a sense of well-being and even elation as you continue fasting and praying, seeking God's face.[60] Fasting draws us nearer to God, revealing our sin-hardened hearts, and leading us to godly repentance.

God leads certain people to extended fasts at times (Matthew 4:1-2, Daniel 10). However, an extended fast (over one to two weeks) should be only at God's specific direction, powered by the grace of the Holy Spirit. We as humans can't go without eating or drinking for long periods of time unless God's Spirit sustains us. Each time we fast, we need to ask God to help us in our weakness. Your flesh will be screaming for gratification. Initially, you will keep thinking of how hungry you are. Ask God for grace and self-control. The Bible speaks of a fast which pleases God.[61] It really does no good to fast if we are so irritable that we are angry and snapping at everyone around us. A fast is no excuse for being rude to people. As my husband told me one time when I was fasting and very irritable, "Go eat something!"

When we fast, the goal is to draw nearer to God and others. Drinking plenty of water and other fluids helps with hunger pains during the fast. You can also fast only from meats and desserts, eating vegetables and drinking water.

---

[60] *7 Basic Steps to Successful Fasting and Praying*, Bill Bright, New Life Publications, Orlando, FL, 1995, p. 7.
[61] Isaiah 58:5, NKJV Bible.

This is called the "Daniel fast," and it is based on Daniel 1. Some people choose to fast food, but also drink fruit juices, sip broth, or eat a little of vegetable soups (this would *not* include beef stew!) Fasting means not eating, and can also mean not drinking anything, but this type of fast requires a special directive from God, because our bodies require water. I usually drink a great deal of water or juice when I fast. It helps with the hunger pains and keeps you hydrated. Since I love coke and coffee, these are hard for me to not drink on the fast. When I obey, I can certainly hear God's voice much more clearly. Caffeine and sugar are usually the hardest addictions to break away from the first few days when fasting. You may experience headaches if you are addicted to caffeine, or if your diet is normally high in sugar. It's a good idea to avoid any type of over-the-counter medication when you are fasting unless it is doctor-recommended. The medicines do not mix well with an empty stomach. I also personally recommend not taking vitamins during a fast. On one particular fast, I was in a great deal of pain after taking two Vitamin C tablets. A few days without vitamins will not hurt you.

Your body actually benefits from fasting. The physical discomforts will pass after awhile, and you will begin to feel great. A side benefit, though it certainly should never be your motive, is that you may lose some weight on the fast. Fasts may make you more aware of your own poor eating habits. You may determine to eat healthier after a fast, because you feel so much better—less water retention, less bloated. It's also a good way to "clean out the pipes" – even better than laxatives. Your body is releasing all those toxins. You just feel clean inside and out after fasting. You truly have a heightened awareness of God's presence when you fast. It is the ultimate high! At times, God may give you dreams, visions, and prophetic words. It is important to record these, and you might submit them to your church leadership. Most of the time, these are personal words to help you in your walk with God. But some dreams or prophecies may be a word for someone in your church or a corporate word. God spoke to Daniel about the end times for nations during his three-week fast.[62] It's a good practice any time you are struggling with some sin in your life, when you need a specific directional word from the Lord, or when you have been under heavy demonic attack to fast and pray. Satan hates fasting and prayer, because he knows it empowers believers to hear God's voice more clearly. He will do everything he can to tempt you to eat or to distract you during the fast so be prepared! Stay in the Word of God, put on worship tapes, pray fervently and put on God's armor each day. Ask the Lord to speak clearly to you and for strength during times of hunger. Satan tempted Jesus when he had not eaten for 40 days in the desert, telling him to turn the stones into

---

[62] Daniel Chapters 10-12, NKJV Bible.

bread.[63] We're fighting against powers and rulers of darkness[64], and need to "pray it through," as the Pentecostals like to say.

My Assembly of God friend Doris Goddard has taught me this expression. It means to persevere in prayer until God's answer comes! Hearing God's voice really just means one thing: active listening. Getting quiet before Him. Turn off the T.V. Get alone. Tune out all distractions. Be still. Be quiet. He will speak to you. You can't hear Him if you're gabbing all the time! Our lives are daily bombarded with noise: television, radio, traffic, road and building construction, and in some places, the sounds of war and violence. We must learn to listen for God's voice. Jesus said to go into your secret place of prayer, and to shut the door.[65] It is only when our hearts are quiet and attentive that we can hear God's voice. If we wait on Him, He will speak to us. If we seek Him, we will find Him.[66] Listen. He's speaking very quietly right now. What is He saying to you?

---

[63] Matthew 4:1-4, NKJV Bible.
[64] Ephesians 6:10-18, NKJV Bible.
[65] Matthew 6:4-6, NKJV Bible.
[66] Matthew 7:7, NKJV Bible.

Chapter Four
Answered Prayer

God has answered so many prayers throughout my life. He has been so good to me, so faithful. If there is one thing I am certain of in this life, it is that God is real, God is good, and God answers prayer. That doesn't mean that my life has been perfect and nothing has ever gone wrong. In fact, I have had my share of suffering in this life. I was abused as a child, in adulthood I had many stormy, painful relationships with men, and I've seen both of my children suffer emotionally and physically due to past medical problems. God miraculously spared my life in three head-on collisions, healed me of a severe eye infection that could have lead to blindness, and delivered me of panic attacks and suicidal depression. He truly has given me beauty for ashes, and a mantle of joy for the spirit of heaviness.[67]

---

[67] Isaiah 61:3, NKJV Bible.

God has been there for me through everything in my life. All that I had to do was call on Him in my hour of need. I want to talk here about answered prayer. I have explained it very simply to our children. Sometimes God says yes, sometimes God says no, and sometimes God says wait. God does *not* say *maybe*! However, sometimes His yes answer is conditional upon our obedience to Him, based on Deuteronomy 11. Our daughter Leah is very strong-willed. She does not like for Ray and me to tell her no. But sometimes we must deny her request for her own good.

God is this way with His children. The Bible says all good gifts are from God.[68] Just as a father or mother would not give their child a stone if he asked for bread, or a snake if he asked for fish, God does not give His children bad gifts.[69] "How much more your Heavenly Father will give good things to those who ask Him!" [70] God is not an angry, withholding, too strict God. We must understand then, that, God's no is answered prayer! We may not like it. We might kick and scream about it. God is not being cruel. He knows what is best for us. Looking back over the years, I thank God for His no answers!

Sometimes it seems like God is silent on matters. This is the time to press in. Study the Bible. Pray. Fast. It may be a timing issue. God always answers right on time. I

---

[68] James 1:17, NKJV Bible.
[69] Matthew 7:10, NKJV Bible.
[70] Matthew 7:9-11, NKJV Bible.

have found Him to sometimes be a last-minute God, but He's never too late. One time my husband Ray and I had to find a place to live. The beautiful Victorian home that we had been renting for two years was going to be sold by the owners, because they were pursuing missions work and did not have time to take care of the rental house. We were given a date to move. It seemed all the odds were against us. One setback was that financially, we were strapped. There also seemed to be a lack of housing in the area with enough rooms for our three children, and that were within our budget! When we had only a week to move, and all the boxes were packed, I was beginning to get nervous. Would we wind up on the street? I had visions of our family eating meals and sleeping in our car, but I kept praying. Three days before we had to have all our belongings out of the Victorian house, we found a three-bedroom, brand-new duplex that was affordable. The landlord even allowed us to pay part of the deposit in the next month's rent. People from our church helped us to load boxes onto trucks and trailers, and we moved into our new home, praising God. God is a last-minute God. He will come through for you!

God will answer your prayers. No request is too small or unimportant for Him. Sometimes I send up little, urgent requests that must amuse God. "Lord, I've lost my key ring again. Please help me to remember where it is!" No request is too big, either. My husband Ray has suffered a lot physically with kidney stones over the years. One time he was passing one that was large and very painful. I went on my knees to intercede on his behalf. I asked God to pulverize that stone, and to smash it into pieces. Soon afterward, Ray passed the stone. After passing the kidney stone, Ray has a habit of saving it for his physician for testing. However, before he would take the stone to the doctor, he would show it to me, while explaining how passing a kidney stone is like having a watermelon pass through a drinking straw. I think he does this for attention and compassion. I've given birth to two children and know what real pain is, but I do murmur a sympathetic, "I'm sorry. I'm glad you are better now." This time, the stone had broken up into tiny pieces, enabling him to pass them much more easily. God answered my prayer to smash that big stone into pieces! "I cry out to God Most High, to the God who does everything for me. He sends help from heaven and saves me. He punishes those who chase me. God sends me His love and truth. God is supreme over the skies; His majesty covers the earth."[71]

Our oldest daughter Heather married Kyle six years ago. Soon after they married, she conceived and became pregnant with our precious, first grandbaby, Annabelle. During her pregnancy, Heather developed pre-eclampsia and other complications. She was referred to a specialist because a sonogram showed fluid around the baby's

---

[71] Psalm 57:2-3, 5, New Century Version Bible.

abdomen, which wasn't normal. Doctors were certain that the baby had either genetic defects or Down's Syndrome. Kyle, Heather, and all of the family members stood firm in trusting God's word, and prayed for miraculous healing of the baby. Annabelle was delivered by C-section, on September 3, Heather's birthday. She was a beautiful, perfectly healthy baby! Heather's midwives, the specialists, and the hospital staff were in awe of Kyle's and Heather's relentless faith throughout this trial. God answers prayer! One of the hardest things for us as Christians to deal with is when the answer to prayer seems delayed. As I said before, God's timing is never too late. It is always perfect. There are several reasons why we don't have the petitions yet, that we have asked God for in prayer: First, we must search our hearts to see if there is any unconfessed sin in our lives. Jeremiah 14:7 (New Century Version) says that, "We know that we suffer because of our sins. We have left you many times; we have sinned against you." James 5:16 tells us to confess our faults, so we may be healed. "It is your evil that has separated you from your God. Your sins have caused Him to turn away from you, so He does not hear you."[72]

If we confess our sins, God will hear us and will forgive us. David knew to cry to God for help. "Lord, hear my

---

[72] Isaiah 59:2, New Century Version Bible.

prayer, and listen when I ask for mercy. I call to you in times of trouble, because You will answer me."[73] The second reason we may not see our prayers being answered is because of strife in our homes. The Bible says that unity brings God's blessing.[74] Husbands and wives need to be in unity or their prayers will be hindered.[75] But the prayer of agreement releases God's answer. "Also, I tell you that if two of you on earth agree about something and pray for it, it will be done for you by my Father in heaven. This is true because if two or three people come together in My name, I am there with them."[76] Forgive others. Come into unity, and agree! Another obstacle to answered prayer is unbelief. Faith can't operate where there is doubt or fear. "Without faith no one can please God." [77] Jesus rebuked His disciples for their unbelief during a fierce storm on the sea: That evening, Jesus said to his followers, "Let's go across the lake."

Leaving the crowd behind, they took Jesus in the boat and a very strong wind came up on the lake. The waves came over the sides and into the boat so that it was already full of water. Jesus was at the back of the boat, sleeping with his head on a cushion. His followers woke him and said, "Teacher, don't you care that we are drowning!" Jesus

---

[73] Psalm 86:7, New Century Version Bible.

[74] Psalm 133:1, NKJV Bible.

[75] 1 Peter 3:7, NKJV Bible.

[76] Matthew 18:19-20, New Century Version Bible.

[77] Hebrews 11:6, New Century Version Bible.

stood up and commanded the wind and said to the waves, "Quiet! Be still!" Then the wind stopped, and it became completely calm. Jesus said to his followers, "Why are you afraid? Do you still have no faith?" The followers were very afraid and asked each other, "Who is this? Even the wind and the waves obey him!"[78] Where is *your* faith? Notice that Jesus was not in denial that there was a problem. God has not included anything in the Bible that isn't important. The Bible says that the disciples were in real danger. These men were fishermen. They were used to storms on the sea. A little rain and lightning weren't going to cause them to be afraid. But this must have been some storm for rough fishermen to feel afraid for their lives! The boat was quickly filling up with water. The wind was howling, and the waves were crashing over the ship. They were at risk of drowning in the ocean. Jesus was peacefully asleep! Christ knew who He was in God. He knew His authority. He stood up, rebuked the winds and the waves, and they stopped! All was calm at His word of authority.

Where is your faith? Only faith pleases the Lord. Only faith moves God. Repent of unbelief and fear, and ask God to fill you with the gift of faith. Faith comes by hearing the Word of God.[79] A fourth reason we do not see immediate results in prayer is because we have an enemy,

---

[78] Mark 4:35-41, New Century Version Bible.
[79] Romans 10:17, NKJV Bible.

Satan, who resists us. When Daniel prayed to God for understanding and for God to release his will over Israel, an angel was sent to speak to him, but was fought hard by the demonic prince of Persia. The archangel Michael was dispatched to help the angel so he could be released to go to Daniel and explain the vision of the end times to him.[80] Satan and his army aggressively fight the people of God. In the case of a delayed answer, we must ensure that our heart is cleansed of any known sin, while bringing our faith and prayers in agreement with God's Word. Especially, when we are prayer for the salvation of a loved one, we must persevere in prayer.

The book of Revelation tells us that there are bowls in heaven filling with the prayers of the saints. When the bowls are full, God answers with fire! The apostle John describes this powerful vision of what happens in heaven: "And I saw the seven angels who stand before God and to whom were given seven trumpets. Another angel came and stood at the altar, holding a golden pan for incense. He was given much incense to offer with the prayers of all God's holy people. The angel put this offering on the golden altar before the throne. The smoke from the incense went up from the angel's hand to God with the prayers of God's people. Then the angel filled the incense pan with fire from the altar and threw it on the earth, and there were flashes of lightning, thunder, and loud noises,

---

[80] Daniel 10:10-20, NKJV Bible.

and an earthquake."[81]   Dutch Sheets, author, pastor in Colorado Springs, CO, and founder of Dutch Sheets Ministries, says our prayers are "God's Holy Detonators": "...we have weapons that are "divinely powerful" to pull down strongholds, if we would only realize it. God says, "Instead of using yours, I'll let you use Mine. Yours won't work, Mine will." The word "powerful" is *dunatos* and is actually one of the New Testament words for a miracle. These weapons empowered by God will work miracles. The word is also translated "possible." I like that. Do you have anything that seems impossible?   Will it take a miracle? With this power, they become possible. And, of course, this is the Greek word from which we get the word dynamite.   This stuff is explosive!   This dynamite is explosive for the "destruction of fortresses" or, as the *King James* translation says, is capable of "pulling down strong-holds.   "Destruction" and "pull down" are the word *kathairesis.* This important and powerful word has a couple of pertinent meanings. One of them is "to bring down with violence or demolish." With this powerful, miracle working dynamite behind our weapons, we can become demolition agents violently tearing down Satan's strongholds."[82]

---

[81] Revelation 8:2-5, New Century Version Bible.
[82] *Intercessory Prayer*, Dutch Sheets, Regal Books, March 3, 2008, p. 169.

Smith Wigglesworth was a great, faith-filled man with a powerful healing ministry in the early 1900's. He took his calling from God very seriously, and did not mess around with the devil. Here he shares a story: "One day a pet dog followed a lady out of her house and ran all around her feet. She said to the dog, "My dear, I cannot have you with me today." The dog wagged its tail and made a big fuss. She said, "Go home, my dear." But the dog did not go. At last she shouted roughly, "Go home," and off it went. Some people deal with the Devil like that. The Devil can stand all the comfort you like to give him. Cast him out! You are not dealing with the person; you are dealing with the Devil. Demon power must be dislodged in the name of the Lord."[83] It is very important to continue to pray when the answer seems delayed. Don't give up. Don't give in to Satan's lies that God does not hear your prayers, or that He won't give you what He has promised.

Four years ago, Ray and I were praying for our daughter Leah, 11 years old at the time, to be healed of sporadic, grand mal seizures that had begun suddenly one night. Her neurologist opted to not put her on medication due to the side effects and because her seizures were sporadic, never occurred during the daytime, and were spreading out and becoming shorter during the last year. They occurred about once a month, during the middle of the night, and she would scream out just before she had one, jolting us out of

---

[83] *Smith Wigglesworth on Spiritual Gifts*, Smith Wigglesworth, Whitaker House, New Kensington, PA, 1998, p. 96.

our sleep. It was a living nightmare for two years for our family. God had promised Ray and me that Leah was healed. We and so many others stood on the Word of God in faith, awaiting the manifestation of that healing to come to pass. God gave me confirmation after confirmation of her healing. We had many people pray over Leah for her healing. Ray and I repented of strife that may have opened the doorway for the enemy to come in, and asked God to forgive us of any sins, so that our daughter would be healed.

We believed that 2005 was the year of her healing. I continued to pray with Leah every night for her healing. She has been a Christian since she was four years old, and believed that Jesus was her healer and deliverer. Every night she prayed in her sweet, little voice, "God, please let me never, never, never have another seizure again! Amen!" When she had the seizures, she was not aware of what was going on, but afterward she would suffer with terrible headaches, nausea and vomiting. She would often cry, and so would I. It was the most helpless feeling I'd ever experienced in my entire life, and I would beg God to heal her. God taught me so much during that time about faith— He taught me how to let go, how to persevere and how to unify with my husband in prayer. God surrounded me with family and friends during that time to help hold me up in prayer. Ray, his parents, our daughters Heather and Eden, my sister Maria Willis, our pastors Lawrence and Louise Wilson, Crystal Tinsley, Pam Thompson, Betty Spangler, Suzy Bunton, Doris Goddard, Royce and Brenda Wilson, Roger and Karen Schroeder, Darin and Tamara Schroeder, Morris and Blanch Hershberger, Don and Gala Palmgren, and so many others at our church. The seizures were spreading further out, and were not lasting nearly as long as when they first began. Her doctor said he thought she would soon outgrow them. Finally, after two years of praying and believing for a miracle, a friend of ours, Frances Lawrence, asked our whole family out one day to eat Chinese food. She also invited us to go to her senior citizen housing apartment to anoint Leah with oil, and believe for her complete healing. Frances is a prayer warrior and a woman of strong faith. We prayed as we had done so many other times, and she anointed Leah with oil. I had been having several dreams that Leah was healed, and received them as a word from God. After Frances prayed, she proclaimed Leah was healed.

After two years, the bowls in heaven of the prayers of the saints were full, and God answered all the prayers of faith on Leah's behalf with His holy fire![84] Jesus Christ healed our little girl. Leah has been seizure free for two years! All glory and honor belong to Lord Jesus Christ! If you are waiting for a prayer to be answered, keep praying. Believe God's word! Persevere. Whatever you do, don't

---

[84] Revelation 5:8, NKJV Bible.

stop! Keep praying. God answers prayer! "It is not yet time for the message to come true, but that time is coming soon, the message will come true. It may seem like a long time, but be patient and wait for it, because it will surely come; it will not be delayed."[85]

---

[85] Habakkuk 2:3, NKJV Bible.

Chapter Five

God's Ways are Not Ours

Several years ago there was a man in our church congregation, Henry, who passed away. He had a massive heart attack years before his death. Doctors did not think he would live long. Henry fooled them. It wasn't his time to die yet! His faithful wife Ramona found a full-time job and supported them, since Henry was not able to work anymore. Meanwhile, Henry grew spiritually in the Word, through a class at church on inner healing called Oaks of Righteousness, and by becoming a helper in our kids' church. The children loved Henry, and he loved them. Then Henry began to get sick again. He was hospitalized several times. Our church prayed for him, standing in the gap for an extended life. The children prayed for Henry. They made a giant "Get Well" card for him when he was in the hospital. It seemed that Henry was going to be okay, because he went home, feeling better. But soon, Henry died and went to his heavenly home.

This was devastating to many family and friends. God's ways are not our ways.[86] Probably one of the issues of life that Christians ask the most questions about concerns healing. Why is it that sometimes God does not heal people? I had a friend, Anita Gail, who was diagnosed with cancer. She was a new believer. She and many others believed that she was going to be miraculously healed. She had finally found and married the man of her dreams, and they envisioned a long, happy life together. Yet, after a time of suffering from re-occurring cancer, she died. Why? Was it a lack of faith? Should people have prayed harder and longer? We don't understand God's ways. As our previous pastor Lawrence Wilson says, in Anita's and Henry's case, they did receive their healing in heaven. That is the ultimate healing, because there is no sickness or disease in heaven.[87]

Pastor Lawrence exhorted us that on this side of eternity, it is our job to just believe and pray for the person to be healed in this life. It is our responsibility to agree with the Word of God and pray for them to recover: I Peter 2:24 says, "Christ carried our sins in His body on the cross so we would stop living for sin and start living for what is right. And you are healed because of His wounds."

---

[86] Isaiah 55:8, NKJV Bible.
[87] Revelation 21:4, NKJV Bible.

We must continue to proclaim and believe that by His stripes we are healed! Don't lose hope or faith!

There are times people do get sick and even die, such as in Henry's or Anita's case. We don't understand why these things happen. But we have to just keep trusting God in faith, leaving the final outcome for everything in life up to Him. There are other situations that make us wonder why God doesn't seem to answer our prayers. The Holocaust, the tragedy of abortion in our land, the events of the 9/11 horror in America all seem to indicate that God must be taking a vacation somewhere. Doesn't He hear our prayers? Why isn't He answering our petitions? Our former pastor's house was robbed one night while he was teaching Wednesday night Bible study at our church! Where was God? Why did He allow this to take place while His servant was doing His work on earth?

We need to remember nothing takes God by surprise. He's still in control and on the throne. All things will work together for our good and His glory.[88] Later our pastor used the situation to preach a great sermon on how Satan steals, kills, and destroys. Sometimes, we simply must persevere in prayer. I believe this applies to situations like removing abortion from our land, or for salvation of our loved ones. It may take a seemingly long time for the answer, but time is not a problem for God. For an entire year, I prayed every night with Leah for my husband Ray to

---

[88] Romans 8:28, NKJV Bible.

get a new job. He was working 24-hour shifts at a fire station as a paramedic-firefighter. The stressful job did not allow him much sleep on his shifts. He went on many 3 a.m. ambulance or fire calls during his seven years there. The kids and I wanted him home at night with us. It seemed as if the heavens were brass! But we continued to pray to God for a new job for Ray. God answered our prayers, far above our expectations. He got a new job as a deputy fire chief, with better pay, family insurance, a new Explorer truck to take home, a cell phone, and other job perks. But it took an entire year of prayer before it came to pass! He is now in a brand new job with even better pay and benefits than his fire chief job. Don't stop praying!

God's ways are above our ways. We need to learn to submit to His will. Sometimes we or loved ones will have financial problems, medical problems, problems at work, problems in the ministry, lose jobs, be relocated to another part of the country, get sick, or die. In the garden of Gethsemane, Jesus prayed earnestly to the Lord, his sweat becoming like drops of blood: "Abba, Father! You can do all things. Take away this cup of suffering. But do what you want, not what I want."[89] We know that it is God's will that all people be saved, serving and intimately knowing Him. But sometimes it seems like God doesn't care that

---

[89] Mark 14:36, Contemporary Version Bible.

people are doing wrong. We may have a spouse who is involved in blatant sin, and feel as if God is not hearing our prayers. "Why won't you do anything about this, God?" we ask Him. As Stormie O'Martian points out in her wonderful, inspired book, *The Power Of A Praying Wife*, prayer does not change others. It changes us.[90] God may be allowing that situation of sin in your loved one's life to expose your own heart of judgment or unforgiveness. When you can truly release that person into God's hands, and get out of the way of the Holy Spirit, then God can and will move in miraculous ways.

I have a friend whose husband became addicted to internet pornography. For many years she suffered great emotional pain, betrayal, and humiliation, as he was pulled deeper into the darkness of perversion and he began forcing her to do things she did not want to do. Her husband's addiction was very destructive to their marriage. My friend discovered pornography on their computer and destroyed it. Her husband found out, became very angry, threatened to hurt her—which resulted in him being shot and killed after fleeing from police in a high-speed car chase. The wages of sin is death.[91] Why didn't God do a miracle and deliver this man from this sin? God gives all of us free choice. We could not serve Him in true worship

---

[90] *The Power Of a Praying Wife*, Stormie O'Martin, Harvest House Publishers, January 1, 2007.
[91] Romans 6:23, NKJV Bible.

and love Him with no choice. We would just be robots. Yet God allowed this terrible tragedy. It brought incredible pain to their family. Their shattered lives are still healing years later. It was never God's will that the husband become addicted to pornography. Nor was the Lord pleased that he died this violent death in life, missing the destiny God desired for Him. But God *allowed* this tragedy, and can even turn this evil into something good for His glory. I believe that one day this heartbreak will be part of my friend's testimony, and she will be able to minister to other women who have gone through the same pain she has endured—the pain of pornography and the pain of a husband's untimely death. Romans 5:20-21 (NKJV) says, "But where sin abounded, grace abounded much more."

I have a friend whose teenage daughter was in a terrible car wreck, and almost died. She suffered a serious head injury, a punctured lung, and broken bones, and was in the hospital for a couple of months. Initially doctors were not sure if she was going to live through the first week. Her mom Reena, and our entire church rallied around Marcy and prayed for miraculous healing. When I visited her in the hospital after her wreck, I was horrified at what I saw. One eye was swollen the size of a golf ball. She was hooked up to all kinds of monitors, and was in a semi-coma state. Here was my friend's daughter and one of our two daughter's closest friends, on the verge of death. I cried all the way driving home, just crying out for God to do a miracle. Her mother Reena was very strong in faith during this time. She did not receive any of the doctor's negative reports, and continued to believe for total healing. God intervened on Marcy's behalf, and she is a walking miracle today, normal in every way. This situation is now part of hers and her family's testimony to the power of Jesus Christ. God took what the enemy intended for evil, and turned it around for His glory. God's ways are not our ways, and His thoughts are not like our finite, human, fleshly ones. His ways are higher than the heavens. We must yield to God and pray as Jesus did, "But do what You want, not what I want." Yes Lord, YOUR will be done!

Chapter 6
The Price

In a book on walking with God, there is a final word I want to share. There is a cost to truly live the yielded life to God and to walk with Him in deep, fulfilling intimacy. There is a price to fulfilling our higher calling, our destiny in Christ. That price is obedience. Most of my life, I have not obeyed God. I was abused as a child, and as I grew up, anger and rebellion to authority grew inside of me. Although I was saved at 18 years old, I walked away from God, and rebelled against Him throughout my 20's. I thank God that He was so loving and faithful, and was willing to take me back after I'd lived in the pig pen of sin! I truly hit the bottom of the barrel before I realized how much I needed Jesus and repented. I learned the hard way how costly sin is, and how devastating its consequences.

I wish I had not wasted years sinning against God and hurting others. If I could give our children one gift, it would be the knowledge of how much God loves them and the importance of obeying Him. I am so thankful to Jesus that the sins of my past are forgiven, and that God has removed them as far as the east is from the west.[92]

It is so much better to avoid sin, than to have to repent of it and then pay the hard consequences of it. We may be forgiven of our sins, but have to suffer the aftermath of our poor choices. David repented of his sin of adultery with Bathseba, but the child they had together died. His home was filled with strife, distrust, bitterness, hatred and betrayal. For the rest of his days, David struggled to keep his king's crown.[93] This was all the consequences of his sin of adultery. The fruit of sin is rotten! It is death to our souls. How much better to live in obedience to God's word and receive His blessings, His goodness, and His favor!

Obey the commands of the Lord your God, living as He has commanded you and respecting Him. "The Lord your God is bringing you into a good land, a land with rivers and pools of water, with springs that flow in the valleys and hills, a land that has wheat and barley, vines, fig trees, pomegranates, olive oil, and honey. It is a land that will have plenty of food, where you will have everything you need. If you ever forget the Lord your God and follow

---

[92] Psalm 103:12, NKJV Bible.
[93] 1 Samuel, NKJV Bible.

other gods and worship them and bow down to them, I warn you today that you will be destroyed." [94] If we obey God, we will be richly blessed! One of the greatest ways we can walk in obedience to God is to love and to forgive others. Don't hold offenses. Don't judge. Don't let the sun go down on your anger. Laugh with, enjoy, and love others. Don't take people for granted. Appreciate them. Tell them, "I love you!" The Bible says that loving God means obeying His commands.[95] Those who continue to sin do not belong to God, but belong to the evil one.[96] If we love God, we will not continue to sin. God's command to us can be summed up in 2 John 6, NKJV: "This is the message that you heard from the beginning, that we should love one another." To love others, we have to receive God's love.

The only way we will ever have that love of God is to spend time with Him, in His presence and in His word. Pray. Find time to be alone with God, and listen to Him. Put on a worship tape. Sit at Jesus' feet, as Mary of Bethany did, and learn from Him. As you are quiet before Him, God will fill you up to overflowing with His Love. He will then empower you to take that Love to a dying and lost world that so desperately needs Him. What all of us as

---

[94] Deuteronomy 8:6-9, 19, New Century Version Bible.
[95] 1 John 5:3, New Century Version Bible.
[96] 1 John 5:18, NKJV Bible.

humans really need is love. God is Love.[97] Our strength for everything we will have to go through in this life can only come from God. There will be difficulties and very dark times ahead. The Bible tells us this. I believe we are now beginning to experience the birth pangs before Jesus' return. We will need to be "prayed up" as the Pentecostals say. My friend Nicki Cantrell had a word from the Lord one time that we need to turn off our televisions, and to cover our windows and homes with prayer. We need to hear God's voice for the times that are coming. Most of all, we need a revelation today of God's love for us. He loved us so much that He sent Jesus to die for our sins. No matter what sin we have done, or that we do now or in the future, we can't ever make God stop loving us. He will always love us. He will never leave us or forsake us.[98] Underneath us are God's everlasting arms of Love.[99] We are always secure in God's arms. Even in the midst of troubles and persecution, God's love will sustain us!

The reason we need to pray is so that we can come to understand how deeply God loves us. "Deep calls unto deep at the noise of your waterfalls."[100] I Corinthians 2:10 speaks of the deep things of God. "But God has shown us these things through the Spirit. The Spirit searches out all things, even the deep secrets of God." God wants to show

---

[97] 1 John 4:8, NKJV Bible.
[98] Hebrews 13:5, NKJV Bible.
[99] Deuteronomy 33:27, NKJV Bible.
[100] Psalm 42:7, NKJV Bible.

you His deep love. He wants to give you His wisdom and His specific plan for your life. You have a great destiny to fulfill! You don't want to miss it! As we pray, God will bring us to a greater understanding of His love and His plan. His love is an unquenchable, burning flame for us.[101] Yes, Jesus loves you, as the children's song says. The Bible does tell us so, but Jesus wants to tell you so Himself. He's inviting you today to come into His presence in prayer. He wants you to take His hand, and just let Him hold you awhile. Walk with Him like this every day, intimately. Talk with Him. Listen to His still, small voice. Do you hear Him? He is whispering to you right now of His love for you.

Beth D. Jones

---

[101] Song of Solomon 8:6, NKJV Bible.

Irie Chobie with a Pistol.
This woodblock print, by the artist Toyokuni (1769-1825), is the only known picture of a kabuki actor with a pistol.

Noel Perrin

Giving Up the Gun
Japan's Reversion
to the Sword, 1543-1879

SHAMBHALA

BOULDER · 1980

Shambhala Publications, Inc.
1920 Thirteenth Street
Boulder, Colorado 80302

A portion of this book appeared in *The New Yorker*
November 20, 1965, under the title 'Giving Up the Gun.'
The author is grateful for permission to reprint.

Distributed in the United States by Random House
and in Canada by Random House of Canada, Ltd.

Library of Congress Cataloging in Publication Data
Perrin, Noel.
Giving up the gun.
Reprint of the ed. published by D. R. Godine, Boston.
Bibliography: p.
1. Japan—History—Period of civil wars,
1480-1603. 2. Japan—History—Tokugawa period,
1600-1868. 3. Firearms, Japanese—History.
4. Swordplay—Japan—History. I. Title.
DS868.2.P47 1980 952 80-50744
ISBN 0-87773-184-5 (pbk.)
ISBN 0-394-73949-3 (Random House)

Printed in the United States of America

FOR MISHIMA YUKIO,
no pacifist, but a long-time hater of guns.

Alas! Can we ring the bells backward? Can we unlearn the arts that pretend to civilize and then burn the world? There is a march of science; but who shall beat the drums for its retreat?
Charles Lamb[1]

You can't turn back the hands of the clock.
Erle Stanley Gardner[2]

I am not of course suggesting any reform; for we can no more go back from poison [gas] to the gun than we can go back from the gun to the sword.
Lord Dunsany[3]

FOREWORD

This book tells the story of an almost unknown incident in history. A civilized country, possessing high technology, voluntarily chose to give up an advanced military weapon and to return to a more primitive one. It chose to do this, and it succeeded. There is no exact analogy to the world's present dilemma about nuclear weapons, but there is enough of one so that the story deserves to be far better known.

To follow the story, the reader needs to know a very little bit of Japanese history. The Japanese have had high culture and advanced technology (of a preindustrial sort) since roughly the eighth century of the Christian era. For the next 850 years the country developed completely independently of Europe, but along somewhat similar lines. It grew to be a feudal society, complete with knights in armor. Better armor, incidentally, than Europeans possessed. It had a code of chivalry. It had a complex religious establishment and many monasteries, most of them in the warlike tradition of the Knights Templar rather than the pacific tradition of the Little Brothers of St. Francis. It had great wealth. It did not have guns.[1]

Guns arrived in 1543, brought by the first Europeans. They were adopted at once, and were used widely for the next hundred years. Then they were gradually abandoned. The adoption was amply witnessed, but not the abandonment. The reason is simple. From 1543 to 1615, foreigners moved freely around Japan. First the Portuguese and then the Spanish, Dutch, and English opened trading stations. The Portuguese and Spanish (but not the Dutch and English) also attempted to convert Japan to Christianity. After some initial successes, they almost completely failed – but not before the Japanese government had become convinced that European missionaries were usually a prelude to European attempts at colonization.[2] The government therefore placed a series of increasingly tight controls, first on missionaries and then on foreigners altogether. From 1616 on, free movement was at an end. The Portuguese and Spanish were required to stay within the city limits of Nagasaki; the Dutch and English were confined to the little port of Hirado.

Even these enclaves proved temporary. In 1623 the English voluntarily gave up their 'factory' at Hirado, because they were losing money. In 1624 the Spanish were expelled from Nagasaki, because they couldn't or wouldn't control their Franciscan missionaries. In 1638 the Portuguese were also expelled. What that left in the way of foreign observers was a handful of Dutchmen. Three years later they virtually ceased to observe, because the Japanese pulled the curtain down on their window. They were not made to leave the country – the Dutch East India Company was too useful in handling trade with China – they were merely put in a kind of limbo. On May 21, 1641, the Dutch were required to give up their shipyards and foundries at Hirado and move to a tiny artificial island in Nagasaki harbor, called Deshima. It was about two hundred yards long by eighty yards wide: just over three acres.

With one annual exception, the Dutch merchants who lived on the island were not allowed to set foot on the mainland, nor were they encouraged to learn Japanese. They saw little and understood less of what went on in Japan during the next two centuries.[3] Certainly they did not understand what happened about guns.

When the first Europeans arrived, Japan consisted of several hundred semi-independent principalities. (The early Europeans regularly referred to the *daimyo* who ruled these principalities as kings.) Technically, all of them were subservient to the emperor in Kyoto – but the mikado's rule was even more of a fiction than that of the Holy Roman Emperor in Germany.

These principalities were almost continuously at war with each other during the first sixty years that Europeans were allowed in Japan. But during that time, three of the most famous leaders Japan has ever had gradually unified the country. These men were Lord Oda Nobunaga, who began the process; Lord Toyotomi Hideyoshi, who all but completed it; and Lord Tokugawa Ieyasu,* who established in 1600 a stable dynasty that lasted until 1867. (Still, of course, technically subservient to the emperor.) Some years before the Tokugawas fell, Japan had been forcibly reopened to foreign trade and foreign technology

---

* These names are backward by Western standards. In Japan, until 1868, the family name came first, and what we call the first name came last. Odo, Toyotomi, and Tokugawa are surnames; Nobunaga, Hideyoshi, and Ieyasu are first names. Since 1868 there has been a gradual though never complete conversion to Western name-order. Japanese first and last names looking much alike to Western eyes, the possibilities for confusion are numerous.

In this book I have followed a simple rule. All Japanese names in the text are family-name-first, even those of the one or two people who lived after 1868. The same is true in the narrative part of footnotes. In book citations and in the bibliography, however, I have followed the standard Western form. In a citation to 'Junji Homma, *The Japanese Sword*,' Junji is the author's first name, Homma his last.

. . . and at that point my brief account can cease. Japan's subsequent history is more or less well known in the West, if not always correctly interpreted.

One final note. The principal European observers in sixteenth-century Japan were Jesuit missionaries, sent by Portugal. Some of them were very capable observers indeed. They read and spoke Japanese with ease, they were highly educated, they were careful and accurate. But they naturally tended to stress religious matters, and to pay relatively little attention to military technology – beyond observing with disgust that their Japanese counterparts, the Buddhist monks, were keen swordsmen and, for a time, formidable users of guns. So even for the period from 1543 to 1615, European accounts tend to be brief and vague on matters of war, full and precise on the number of Christian converts in Owari, the kinds of restrictions placed on missionaries in Kyoto. This is one reason why even now, in the Western memory of that period in Japan, there is general awareness of the expulsion of Christianity, and almost no awareness of either the rise or the abandonment of firearms.

Anyone wanting a full historical account of the period when guns flourished would naturally turn first to C. R. Boxer's *The Christian Century in Japan*. After that, to the great histories of Japan by Murdoch and Sansom. Perhaps then to the book written by Joao Rodrigues, S.J., in 1620, and translated into English by Michael Cooper, S.J., in 1973 as *This Island of Japon*. The reader will not find that history here (nor much about guns there.) In what follows, I have focused almost entirely on the firearms themselves, on rival weapons, on arms manufacture, and on the general question of how one unlearns the use of a weapon.

Noel Perrin
Dartmouth College
April 1979

Giving Up the Gun

ONE

In early January 1855, the U.S.S. *Vincennes*, an eighteen-gun sloop of war under Commander John Rodgers, USN, dropped anchor in the southern bay of Tanegashima Island, twenty miles below Kyushu, at the southern tip of Japan. The *Vincennes* was the flagship of the newly created United States Surveying Expedition to the North Pacific Ocean; she had come to begin a six-month survey of Japanese coastal waters. The Japanese were not at all eager to have foreigners prowling around their islands, but they were powerless to prevent it. Not only did they lack a navy, but just the year before, under the sixty-four-pound guns of Commodore Perry's fleet, they had reluctantly signed the Treaty of Kanagawa, the celebrated 'opening of Japan.' The treaty specifically authorized this survey.

Sometime on January 9th, Commander Rodgers led an armed party ashore on Tanegashima to buy stores. He was poorly equipped for business transactions, having no knowledge of Japanese and no interpreter – having nothing, in fact, but an English-Chinese dictionary. Nevertheless, he did get his wood and water, bargaining for them in sign language. He also got a good look at native life. The thing that impressed him most about the islanders was their almost complete ignorance of ordinary nineteenth-century weapons.

'These people seemed scarcely to know the use of firearms,' he noted in his report to the Secretary of the Navy. 'One of [my] officers caught the Japanese word for gun with which a very learned man was displaying his knowledge to his companions. It strikes an American, who from his childhood has seen children shoot, that ignorance of arms is an anomaly indicative of primitive innocence and Arcadian simplicity. We were unwilling to disturb it.'[4]

In writing his report, Commander Rodgers showed himself to be almost as Arcadianly simple as the Tanegashimans themselves. They were innocent about guns, all right, but it was an acquired innocence, not a primitive one. The ancestors of those islanders had not only used guns but had been the first in Japan to do so, and during the mid-sixteenth century guns were known all over Japan as *tanegashima*. Later the standard name became *teppo*, and this is presumably the word the American officer overheard in 1855. By then the Japanese had moved from swords to guns, and back to swords again. They had learned to cast cannon of a respectable size, and had nearly – but not quite – unlearned the art again. They had fought battles in the late sixteenth century using more guns than any European country possessed.

But of all this Commander Rodgers knew nothing. He didn't even know that his very survey was repeating one done by the Spanish in 1612.[5] Nor is his ignorance surprising. In 1855 no American knew much about Japan. The country had been closed to foreigners for nine generations. The oldest institution in Commander Rodgers's America was Harvard University, founded in 1636 – and *Sakoku*, the Closed Country Policy, was three months older than Harvard. There was little he could have learned from books. The *Encyclopaedia Americana*, if Commander Rodgers had happened to study it before sailing, would have given him four pages of rather garbled information about Japan. The *Bri-*

tannica could have told him more, but not much. That learned work would have informed him that the country was ruled by the descendants of 'Jejessama,' by whom they unquestionably meant Tokugawa Ieyasu. 'Jejes' is an anglicization of 'Ieyasu,' and 'sama' is an honorific. It would be roughly comparable if a Japanese encyclopedia had said that the first president of the United States was a person named 'Honorable George' – or, better yet, 'Honorable Joji,' since this is how 'George' would appear in Japanese.

As to weapons, the *Britannica* would have told Rodgers that in the Japan of 1855 swords were 'the principal and best weapon . . . they are far superior to the Spanish blades so celebrated in Europe. A tolerably thick nail is easily cut in two without any damage to the edge.' [6]

In the matter of cutting nails, the *Britannica* was correct.

Of guns, past or present, he would have learned virtually nothing. The whole story of the Japanese adventure with guns, to the extent that it was ever known in the West, had been pretty well lost over the centuries. Even now it has not been fully recovered.

But one fact is certain. The Japanese were keen users of firearms for nearly a hundred years. They then turned back to swords and spears. Few scholars agree completely on what made them do it, or on how, having gone so far with guns, they were able to retrace their steps. Contemporary accounts are scarce.

·

The story begins clearly enough, however. It starts within a mile or two of where the *Vincennes* anchored in 1855, a little over three centuries earlier. The year was 1543, and a Chinese cargo ship – maybe half the size of the *Vincennes* – had come into that same small harbor. The ship's name, if it ever had one, has been lost. Concerning the hundred men on board, though, much survives. Most of them were Chinese trader-pirates of a type common at the time. One, however, was an educated Chinese sailor whose name appears in Japanese as Goho, and three were Portuguese adventurers, also of a type common at the time. Portugal had had a colony in India since 1510, and Portuguese men and ships were beginning to appear all over the Far East. The three Portuguese rovers aboard this ship are the first Europeans known to have reached Japan.

Two of them had arquebuses and ammunition with them; and at the moment when Lord Tokitaka, the feudal master of Tanegashima, saw one of them take aim and shoot a duck, the gun enters Japanese history. Using Goho as an interpreter, Lord Tokitaka immediately made arrangements to take shooting lessons. Within a month he had bought both Portuguese guns.[7] He is supposed to have paid a thousand taels in gold for each of them – a sum difficult to translate accurately into modern terms. But it was a lot of money. Seventy years later you could buy a good arquebus in Japan for two taels.[8] It's somewhat as if Winchester rifles had originally sold for $10,000 each, and gradually dropped to $20. Sixty years later still, six taels a month was regarded as fair wages for a workingman.

The same day that Tokitaka bought the guns, he ordered his chief swordsmith, a man named Yatsuita Kinbei, to start making copies of them. There is a sad story that Yatsuita, unable to get the spring mechanism in the breech quite right, gave his seventeen-year-old daughter to the captain of a Portuguese ship that arrived some months later, in return for lessons in gunsmithing from the ship's armorer.* Whether that is true or not,

---

* No one should discount the Japanese use of guns on the grounds that 'the Portuguese taught them.' Virtually every country derived its advances in weaponry from abroad. For example, the same year the arquebus arrived in Japan, the cast-iron cannon arrived in England. English cannon had previously all been bronze – high-quality, high-price weap-

The First Gun in Japan.
Hokusai, one of the greatest of all Japanese artists, drew and captioned this picture. 'On August 25, 1543,' his caption reads, 'these foreigners were cast upon the island of Tanegashima in Okuma Province.' The foreigners, the caption continues, were named Murashukusha and Kirishitamota. Murashukusha remains a puzzle, but Kirishitamota is the Christopher (or Antonio) da Mota who was undoubtedly one of the three Portuguese aboard that ship. The real da Mota was not necessarily as dwarfish as Hokusai drew him in 1817. (From Vol. VI of the Mangwa.*)*

it is certain that within a year Yatsuita had made his first ten guns, and that within a decade gunsmiths all over Japan were making the new weapon in quantity. An order for five hundred *tanegashima* put in by Lord Oda Nobunaga in 1549 is still on record.[10] So is an account of the skill with which Japanese samurai quickly learned to use guns. The book called *Teppo-ki* or *History of Guns* describes Lord Tokitaka's drill procedures in the middle 1540s. 'All his vassals from far and near trained with the new weapon,' says *Teppo-ki*; 'and soon, out of every hundred shots they fired, many of them could hit the target a hundred times.'[11]

By 1560, the use of firearms in large battles had begun (a general in full armor died of a bullet wound that year),[12] and fifteen years after that they were the decisive weapon in one of the great battles of Japanese history.

All this represents what would now be called a technological breakthrough. As present-day Japanese writers like to point out, the Arabs, the Indians, and the Chinese all gave firearms a try well ahead of the Japanese, but only the Japanese mastered the manufacturing process on a large scale, and really made the weapon their own.

There were good reasons for Japan's special success. The country was a soldierly one to begin with. As St. Francis Xavier wrote in 1552, after a two-year stay in Japan, 'They prize and honor all that has to do with war, and there is nothing of which they are so proud as of weapons adorned with gold and silver. They always wear swords and daggers, both in and out of the house, and when they go to sleep they hang them at the bed's

ons. But in 1543 a French iron-master named Peter Baude began to teach the metal workers of Sussex how to mass-produce relatively cheap iron cannon. Within thirty years, the iron cannon was an English specialty, and justly famous. But its origin lay in 'foreign technical assistance and foreign workmen.'[9]

head. In short, they value arms more than any people I have ever seen.'[13] St. Francis had seen a good many, beginning with his own warlike relatives in Spain. It is probably fair to say that military glory was the goal of every well-bred male in sixteenth-century Japan, except a handful of court nobles in Kyoto. *Their* goal was literary glory.

Furthermore, at the moment when firearms arrived, Japan happened to be in the middle of a century-long power struggle. The Japanese name for the period from 1490 to 1600 is *Sengoku Jidai*, or Age of the Country at War. Several dozen major feudal lords were vying to get military control of the country, make a puppet of the shogun (the emperor was already the shogun's puppet), and rule. Naturally, such men were interested in new weapons and in anything else that would give them an advantage.

Equally important, Japan had already reached a high level of technology. Her copper and steel were probably better, and were certainly cheaper, than any being produced in Europe at the time. Her copper, indeed, was so cheap that in the seventeenth century it began to be exported all over the world, just as Japanese electronic equipment is now. Despite the enormously high shipping costs in that age of sailing ships, the Dutch, for example, found it profitable to send Japanese copper ten thousand miles to Amsterdam. In Japan it cost them thirty-three florins per hundred pounds, delivered to their docks in Nagasaki. In Amsterdam they sold it at fifty-nine florins – still a shade under the price of Swedish copper at sixty florins.[14] Most Dutch founders preferred it for casting bronze cannon.[15]

In iron and steel, Japan could undersell England. England was the recognized leader among European producers. So much was this the case that in the years just before the Spanish Armada, the Spaniards made frantic attempts to import iron cannon from England to arm the Armada with. And despite an

English embargo, they did get twenty-three black-market cannon in 1583, for a total weight of 13.5 tons of iron.[16]

But when the British East India Company opened a trade center in Japan in 1613 and tried shipping in some ingots, they got nowhere. Here is a mournful excerpt from the Company's year-end trade summary for 1615: '*Coromandel Steel* was in no esteem; some which came in on the *Hoseander* being considered inferior to Japan iron. English iron would sell still worse, the best Japan iron being but 20 mace the picul.'[17] That is, ten shillings for 125 pounds.

Nor was Japan any mere producer of raw materials. She was a great manufacturing country, then as now. She led the world in paper products, for example. One of the Jesuit missionaries estimated that there were ten times as many kinds of paper produced in Japan as in Europe.[18] The list extended to an Oriental version of Kleenex, a product the Japanese were making in bulk at least three centuries before Americans suppose themselves to have invented this useful item. They even exported it. An Englishman named Peter Mundy happened to be in Macao, on the China coast, in 1637, and was much impressed when he saw some Osaka merchants' representatives using it.

'Some few Japoneses wee saw in this Citty,' Mundy later wrote. 'They blow their Noses with a certaine sofft and tough kind of paper which they carry aboutt them in small peeces, which having used, they Fling away as a Fillthy thing, keeping handkerchiefes of lynnen to wype their Faces.'[19] Naturally Mundy was impressed. In England, at the time, most people used their sleeves.

But the thing Japan manufactured most of was weapons. For two hundred years she had been the world's leading exporter of arms. The whole Far East used Japanese equipment. In 1483, admittedly an exceptional year, 67,000 swords were shipped to China alone.[20] A hundred and fourteen years later, a visiting

Italian merchant named Francesco Carletti noted a brisk export trade in 'weapons of all kinds, both offensive and defensive, of which this country has, I suppose, a more abundant supply than any other country in the world.'[21] Even as late as 1614, when things were about to change, a single trading vessel from the small port of Hirado sailed to Siam with the following principal items of cargo: fifteen suits of export armor at four and a half taels the suit, eighteen short swords at half a tael each, twenty-eight short swords at a fifth of a tael, ten guns at four taels, ten guns at three taels, and fifteen guns at two and a half taels.[22]

These were top-quality weapons, too. Especially the swords. A Japanese sword blade is about the sharpest thing there is. It is designed to cut through tempered steel, and it can. Tolerably thick nails don't even make an interesting challenge. In the 1560s one of the Jesuit fathers visited a particularly militant Buddhist temple – the Monastery of the Original Vow, at Ishiyama. He had expected to find the monks all wearing swords, but he had not expected to find the swords quite so formidable. They could cut through armor, he reported, 'as easily as a sharp knife cuts a tender rump.'[23] Another early observer, the Dutchman Arnold Montanus, wrote that 'Their Faulchions or Scimeters are so well wrought, and excellently temper'd, that they will cut our *European* blades asunder, like Flags or Rushes. . . .'[24]

Stories of wonder weapons and superhuman feats abound in sixteenth-century literature, and most of them now seem merely to show what good liars (or how credulous) our ancestors were. They believed in mermaids and the philosopher's stone, too. But Montanus's story can be checked, and has been. The distinguished twentieth-century arms collector George Cameron Stone once took part in a test in which a sixteenth-century Japanese sword was used to cut a modern European sword in two.[25] And there exists in Japan right now a film showing a machine-gun barrel being sliced in half by a sword from the forge of the great fifteenth-century maker, Kanemoto II.[26] If this seems improbable, one must remember that smiths like Kanemoto hammered and folded and rehammered, day after day, until a sword blade contained something like four million layers of finely forged steel. (Or, rather, until the *edge* of the blade did. The rest was of much softer steel. A whole blade made like the edge would be as brittle as glass, and shatter at the first blow. This technique of varying the hardness was one that European smiths never perfected, which is why European swords were never as sharp.) People who could make weapons of this quality were not going to have much trouble adapting their technology to firearms.

Finally, Age of the Country at War or not, Japan was in booming good health. During the sixteenth century it had a larger population than any European country: twenty-five million people, compared to sixteen million in France, seven million in Spain, four and a half million in England, and maybe a million in what is now the United States. Agriculture was flourishing. So was the building industry. A Jesuit named Luis Frois saw Lord Oda Nobunaga's newly built castle at Gifu in 1569, and reacted the way his colleague Gaspar Vilela did to the monks' swords. 'I wish I was a good architect, or had the gift of being able to describe places well,' Father Frois wrote his superior, 'because I assure you emphatically, that among all the palaces and houses which I have seen in Portugal, India, and Japan, I never yet saw anything comparable to this in freshness, elegance, sumptuousness, and cleanliness.'[27]

As for education, the Buddhist monks maintained five 'universities,' the smallest of them larger than the Oxford or Cambridge of the time.[28] And while no exact statistics are available, there is every reason to believe that the general literacy rate was higher in Japan in 1543 than in any European country whatsoever.*

* Certainly this was how it struck the Japanese. They could hardly believe

Interest in the arts ran high, too. Career military officers – that is to say, members of the *bushi* class – were expected to read and quote the classics between battles, while in 1588 the senior military commander in the whole country gave a series of poem parties. A timely poem could sometimes even save a man's life. During a suspected rebellion, for example, a court noble named Lord Tameakira was being held for questioning by the military governor of Suruga, a tough samurai. It was believed that Lord Tameakira knew the whole plot, and that a little judicious torture would make him reveal it. While they were building the fire, Lord Tameakira requested an inkstone and paper. Everybody supposed that he was going to write out a confession, and the paper was promptly brought. Instead he composed a poem.

> *It is beyond belief!*
> *I am questioned not on the art of poetry*
> *But on the things of this transient world!* [30]

The military governor and his staff were so impressed by the elegance of this response that they released Lord Tameakira unharmed.

That incident occurred well before the arrival of guns. But interest in literature had, if anything, increased during the interval. Indeed, Father Organtino Gnecchi, still another missionary stationed in Japan in the late sixteenth century, thought that the general level of culture (religion excepted) was higher than

how widespread illiteracy was among their visitors. In fact they found our ancestors fairly simple in most respects. The earliest Japanese account of the three original Portuguese adventurers is typical. The Japanese chronicler wrote in a superior way, 'They eat with their fingers instead of with chopsticks such as we use. They show their feelings without any self-control. They cannot understand the meaning of written characters. . . . They have no fixed abode, and barter things which they have for those they do not, but withal they are a harmless sort of people.' [29]

back home in Italy.[31] Italy was, of course, at the height of the Renaissance. Don Rodrigo Vivero y Velasco, the retiring Spanish governor of the Philippines, came to much the same conclusion after a visit in 1610.[32] This is not the conclusion that Spaniards came to, for example, in Peru.

TWO

Even in so receptive an environment, firearms naturally did not take over all at once. On the contrary, there was an enormous overlap with existing weapons, and there was plenty of skepticism about guns having any real military value at all. Those five hundred guns ordered by Lord Oda Nobunaga in 1549, for example, represented arms for only a tiny proportion of his troops, and even ten years later he seems to have regarded firearms as a sort of military gimmick. 'Weapons of war have changed from age to age,' he is supposed to have said at a conference with his followers. 'In very ancient times, bows and arrows were the fashion, then swords and spears came into use, and recently guns have become all the rage. These weapons all have their advantages, but I intend to make the spear the weapon on which to rely in battle.'[33] Then he opened a debate on the question of long spears versus short spears.

Lord Oda's skepticism reflected partly the mere newness of firearms in 1559 and partly their primitive nature. The Portuguese arquebus, or the Japanese *teppo*, or the English matchlock was a very slow-firing weapon. Not only did you have to load it from the muzzle, but it took a series of complex motions to arrange the priming. *Very* complex motions. Sir Charles Oman, in his *History of the Art of War in the XVI Century*, quotes a sixteenth-century joke about a matchlockman's frantic motions as he loaded. 'It was said that muskets [that is, large matchlocks] would be more practical if Nature had endowed mankind with three hands instead of two.'[34] According to one sixteenth-century estimate, an archer could shoot fifteen arrows while a matchlockman was loading once.[35] Even that estimate assumes a matchlockman with good physical coordination and some training. The twentieth-century historian of technology John Nef has reckoned that an average or clumsy soldier might take ten to fifteen minutes to load his piece.[36]

He had no very formidable weapon even then. The light bullet that early models carried did damage only up to eighty or a hundred yards, and even inside that range it was likely to bounce off well-made armor. There is a scene in the famous Japanese play *The Battles of Coxinga* (first produced in 1725, but set in the year 1644) in which a loyal nobleman is helping an empress escape. 'Suddenly,' says the play's narrator, 'matchlock fire sweeps down on them like a driving rain from the surrounding woods and mountains. Go Sankei shields the empress, taking bullet after bullet on his stoutly fashioned armor, but – has her destiny run out? – a shot strikes her breast. The jeweled thread of her life is snapped, and she breathes her last.'[37]

Furthermore, in a *real* driving rain a matchlock simply doesn't work. The matchlock gets its name because what happens when you pull the trigger is that a slow-burning match or fuse is brought into contact with the powder. If it's raining, the match won't burn. And the soldiers had no matches of the modern sort with which to relight them.

Europeans encountered these difficulties just as much as the Japanese. On one memorable occasion during the civil wars in France – at La Roche-L'Abeille on June 25, 1569, ten years after Lord Oda's debate – a brisk rain set in just as two groups of matchlockmen were about to shoot it out. They were reduced to clubbing each other over the heads with their wet guns, like so many boys with baseball bats.[38] Japan is a notably rainy country.

Besides these technical difficulties, the Japanese also had a social problem with guns. It had long been the custom in Japanese battles for the soldiers on both sides to exchange ritual compliments before the slaughter began. Sometimes champions on both sides would step forward and boast of their reputations. A very famous early battle near Kyoto began with a champion – a Buddhist monk, as it happens – striding out in front of the army. He was a romantic figure, wearing black armor, and carrying a black sword, a bow, and two dozen black-feathered arrows. The epic tale *Heike Monogatari* describes his next action: 'In a mighty voice he named his name, saying, "You have long heard of me, now take a good look. I am Tsutsui no Jomo Meishu, known to all of Mii Temple as a warrior worth a thousand men." '[39] Only then does he start shooting.

These habits still prevailed in the early days of firearms. When Lord Takeda Harunobu went off to the battle of Uedahara in 1548 – just five years after guns had arrived – he had with him, besides his samurai, two hundred lower-class soldiers. A hundred and fifty were armed conventionally with one sword (samurai, of course, carry two) and a bow and arrows. The other fifty were his secret weapon. Each had a sword and a gun.

But it never occurred to Lord Takeda to change the ritual of battle. As an old account of Uedahara puts it, 'They should have used *tanegashima* first, but they didn't – they started by introducing themselves.'

When the battle began, immediately after the ceremonies, the gunners didn't have time to check their priming and light their matches. This gave the advantage to the enemy, and Lord Murakami Yoshikigo's troops are said to have won 'because they did not have any guns.'[40]

But there were solutions to all these problems, and Japanese generals found them – in the case of some of the technical problems, sooner than European generals. They developed a serial firing technique to speed up the flow of the bullets. They increased the caliber of the guns to increase each bullet's effectiveness, and they ordered waterproof lacquered cases to carry the matchlocks and gunpowder in. They also learned to skip the introductions, and just shoot. Meanwhile, Japanese gunmakers were busy refining the comparatively crude Portuguese firing mechanism – developing, for example, a helical main spring and an adjustable trigger-pull.[41] They also devised a gun accessory – unknown, so far as I am aware, in Europe – which enabled a matchlock to be fired in the rain. In the year of the skirmish at La Roche-L'Abeille (1567), all this had gone far enough so that Lord Takeda (by then known as Takeda Shingen – he changed his name in 1551) could issue a new general order to his retainers, who constituted one of the two or three principal armies in Japan. Twenty-one years had passed since his defeat at Uedahara, and twenty-six since the arquebus had first appeared in the country. 'Hereafter, guns will be the most important arms,' Lord Takeda said. 'Therefore, decrease the number of spears [per unit], and have your most capable men carry guns.'[42]

One proof of Takeda's rightness about the growing impor-

Noel Perrin

How to Use a Matchlock in the Rain.
Waterproof covers to protect the burning match were invented in the seventeenth century – though this picture by Kuniyoshi dates from 1855. The six soldiers, dressed in raincoats, are lower-class ashigaru *– note that each has only one sword, instead of the two that a samurai would carry. The inscription on the picture says that this 'gun accessory' is for use at night as well as during a rainstorm. (It would conceal the glow of the smoldering match.) It also says that a troop of* ashigaru *gunners should always be accompanied by 'a number of well-trained samurai gunmen.' (S. Yoshioka Collection, Kyoto.)*

18

tance of guns is that he himself died of a bullet wound in 1573. But much more important as proof was the Battle of Nagashino, fought between his successor, Takeda Katsuyori, and Lord Oda in 1575. In this battle, Lord Oda, the former devotee of the spear, appeared with an army of 38,000 men, of whom 10,000 were matchlockmen. Of these, the three thousand best trained were the chief cause of his great victory. He never even considered letting them introduce themselves – or even be honorably visible. They were concealed across the Taki River, a narrow stream but still wide enough to slow up charging cavalry.

Not only were they across the river, they were behind breastworks. Lord Oda had them drawn up in three ranks. Like the Americans at Bunker Hill two centuries later, they were told to hold their fire (in this case literally, since each man held a burning match in his hand) until the last instant. Then they were to shoot on command, in volleys of a thousand. Thus, the men in the first rank could be nearly reloaded, and those in the second rank reaching for their bullet pouches, before the third rank ever fired.

It all worked out brilliantly. Takeda's samurai did charge, and they were mowed down. In fact, the plan was so successful that a Japanese lieutenant general writing in 1913 could say that in his opinion very little improvement in infantry tactics had been made since.[44] At Nagashino, incidentally, both sides had a few pieces of light artillery. They were made in Japan, but with the aid of Portuguese advisers. A few months after the battle, the first two cannon made in Japan entirely by Japanese were delivered to Lord Oda for test-firing at Gifu. They were bronze two-pounders, about nine feet long.[45]

It is interesting to compare Nagashino with European battles of the time. In terms of weaponry, the Japanese would appear to have been substantially ahead. (This is true only of field weapons, to be sure. In the use of coast and naval artillery, Europe

Noel Perrin

Gunfire at Nagashino.
*Tokugawa gunners, allied with Lord Oda, are firing across the
Taki River. The tips of the spears of Takeda's charging cavalry
can be seen at the far right.*

    *The man with the antlered helmet in the lower left corner is
Honda Tadakatsu, who historically commanded one of the three
ranks of 1,000 gunners who won the battle. In this seventeenth-
century picture, the number of his gunners is reduced to fourteen for aesthetic reasons. As Yamane Yuzo, the leading authority on Japanese* momoyama *painting says, a battle scene was not
supposed to be 'documentary' or 'realistic'; instead we find a
much simplified and idealized version, with plenty of individual
heroes.*[43] *(Detail from a painted screen, Tokugawa Art Museum, Nagoya.)*

was, and remained, far ahead of Japan.[46]) By comparison, the Battle of Glenlivet, in Scotland, looks distinctly medieval, even though it took place twenty years later. That battle was fought between feudal chiefs not wholly unlike Lord Oda and Lord Takeda. On one side was the young Earl of Argyll – the Argylls didn't become dukes until 1701 – leading the Campbells. On the other was the rebel Earl of Huntly, leading the Gordons. Argyll was supporting James VI of Scotland; Huntly hoped to unseat him. A present-day Scottish historian, T. C. Smout, says their campaign 'involved almost the whole of the northern mainland, and assumed the proportions of a civil war.'[47] Scotland, too, was in an Age of the Country at War.

Lord Argyll brought about ten thousand Highlanders to Glenlivet. Lord Huntly had only two thousand Lowlanders. Despite these odds, he won a stunning victory. Why? Argyll's troops fought mostly with claymores and pikes – that is, swords and spears. But Huntly's small force not only included some matchlockmen, he had artillery – not so much as either side possessed at Nagashino, but quite enough to carry the day in Scotland. If Commander Rodgers wanted to find true Arcadian simplicity, he should have been at Glenlivet, watching the clans. The Campbells were brave men, but wholly unprepared for cannon fire. As J. H. Burton, the late Historiographer-Royal for Scotland, explained the victory, Huntly 'had six field-pieces – an arm which the Highlanders long after this period could never hear without panic."[48]

Scotland was then a backward country. France was the center of European culture. Nevertheless, King Henry IV's victory at Coutras, twelve years after Nagashino, also seems a little primitive by comparison, even though more French gentry perished at Coutras than in any preceding battle of the French civil wars.

There were a great many firearms at Coutras, including two cannon on Henry's side and about seven with the Duc de Joyeuse. But, keeping in mind Lord Oda's army, one finds it hard to be impressed by Henry's stratagem of putting a platoon of twenty-five arquebusiers between each squadron of his spear-bearing cavalry, or even by his three hundred men-at-arms with pistols. These, however, are generally reckoned to have won him the day.[49] They are also supposed to account for the great disparity in casualties – fewer than two hundred men on Henry's side and twenty-seven hundred on the other. At Nagashino, 16,000 died.*

THREE

During the half century after Lord Oda's victory, firearms were at their height in Japan. Not to know how to use them was not to be a soldier. But, at the same time, the first resistance to firearms was developing. It arose from the discovery that efficient

---

* None of these figures is offered as precise. Probably *no* body count, from Cannae through Vietnam, has been very precise. Soldiers exaggerate. There is a famous story about a French general, the Duc de Villars, who lived about a century later than de Joyeuse. Dictating a battle report, de Villars first stated that he had encountered an enemy force of 3,000 men. Then he described his victory. Then, with the ebullience characteristic of

weapons tend to overshadow the men who use them. Prior to Nagashino, the normal Japanese battle had consisted of a very large number of single combats and small melees. After introducing themselves (unless they were gunners), people paired off. Such a battle could produce almost as many heroic stories as there were participants. It even had a kind of morality, since each man's fate depended principally on his own ability and state of training. Equipment counted, too, of course. Defensive armor was considered especially important ('The Japanese made more varieties of mail than all the rest of the world put together,'[51] said George Stone), and a well-made piece of it came in for a full share of praise. In an old description of a battle fought in 1562, there is one incident that reads remarkably like a modern advertisement. Late in the battle, a general named Ota Sukemasa, who had already been wounded twice, got into single combat with an enemy knight named Shimizu.

'His assailant, a man noted for his strength, threw down the now weary and wounded Ota, but tried in vain to cut off his head,' the account runs. 'At this, Ota, his eyes flashing with anger, cried out, "Are you flurried, sir? My neck is protected by a NODOWA [a jointed iron throatpiece]. Remove this, and take off my head."

'Shimizu replied with a bow, "How kind of you to tell me! You die a noble death. You have my admiration!" But just as he was about to remove the NODOWA, two squires of Ota rushed up and, throwing down Shimizu, enabled their master to decapitate his foe and retire safely from the field.'[52]

generals in all ages, he proceeded to put the number of enemy dead at 4,000. When the secretary to whom he was dictating pointed out the statistical difficulty involved, he shrugged and changed the number of those killed to 2,500.[50]

There can be no doubt, however, that far more men died at Nagashino than at Coutras.

Incidents like this occurred very rarely in mass battles with matchlocks. A well-aimed volley of a thousand shots killed flurried soldiers and cool-headed ones without discrimination – and at a distance too great for conversation. Bravery was actually a disadvantage if you were charging against guns, while if you changed sides and became a matchlockman yourself, there was still not much chance for individual distinction. You were now simply one of the thousand men in your rank, waiting behind your breastworks to mow down the charging enemy. It didn't even take much skill to do this. Skill had been moved back from the soldier to the manufacturer of his weapon, and up from the soldier to his commander. Partly for that reason, many of Lord Oda's matchlockmen were farmers and members of the yeoman class called *goshi* or *ji-samurai*, rather than samurai proper. It was a shock to everyone to find out that a farmer with a gun could kill the toughest samurai so readily.

The result was that soon after Nagashino two conflicting attitudes toward guns began to appear. On the one hand, everyone recognized their superiority as long-range killing devices, and all the feudal lords ordered them in large numbers. At least in absolute numbers, guns were almost certainly more common in Japan in the late sixteenth century than in any other country in the world.[53] On the other hand, no true soldier – that is, no member of the *bushi* class – wanted to use them himself. Even Lord Oda avoided them as personal weapons. In the ambush in which he died, in 1582, he is supposed to have fought with his great bow until the string broke, and then with a spear.[54] The following year, during a battle in which something like two hundred ordinary soldiers were hit by artillery fire, the ten acknowledged heroes of the battle made their names with swords and spears.[55]

This attempted division of warfare into upper-class fighting with swords and lower-class fighting with guns did not, of

course, work. The two methods kept colliding. The death of
Lord Mori Nagayoshi, in 1584, is typical. Lord Mori, who was
wearing full armor with a kind of white silk jupon over it, and
who thus made an extremely conspicuous target, persisted in
riding out in front of his troops to rally them. He probably
waved his sword.[56] A matchlockman took careful aim at his head
and knocked him off his horse dead, aged twenty-seven.

That same year, the two leading generals in Japan met with
their armies at a place called Komaki. Both had the lessons of
Nagashino very clearly in mind, and both had a high proportion
of gunners among their troops. The result was an impasse. Not
only were there no introductions and no individual heroics,
neither general would allow his cavalry to attack at all against
the other's guns. Instead, both armies dug trenches, settled in,
and waited, firing an occasional volley or blowing up a few of
the enemy with a land mine to pass the time. In some ways it
was like a scene from World War I, three and a half centuries
ahead of schedule. In the end the two commanders made an
alliance, and went off to fight other armies that were less con-
stricted by their own technology.

A couple of years later, Lord Hideyoshi, the regent of Japan
at the time, took the first step toward the control of firearms. It
was a very small step, and it was not taken simply to protect
feudal lords from being shot by peasants but to get *all* weapons
out of the hands of civilians. What Lord Hideyoshi did was
characteristically Japanese. He said nothing about arms control.
Instead, he announced that he was going to build a statue of
Buddha that would make all existing statues look like midgets.
It would be of wood, braced and bolted with iron. And it would
be so enormous (the figure was about twice the scale of the
Statue of Liberty), that many tons of iron would be needed just
for the braces and bolts.

Still more was required to erect the accompanying temple,

which was to cover a piece of ground something over an eighth of a mile square. All farmers, *ji-samurai*, and monks were invited to contribute their swords and guns to the cause. They were, in fact, required to. As a result, anyone visiting Kyoto in 1587 would have seen a curious scene of disarmament. He would have seen scores of blacksmiths busy hammering matchlocks into religious hardware. The Jesuit Annual Letter for that year reported rather bitterly that Lord Hideyoshi was 'planning to possess himself of all the iron in Japan,' and added, 'He is crafty and cunning beyond belief. Now he is depriving the people of their arms under pretext of devotion to Religion.'[57]

No one was depriving the armies of *their* arms, of course, and the production of guns continued to rise for another twenty years. Lord Hideyoshi himself had a powerful need of them. He had a new plan, which was, briefly, to conquer Korea, China, and then the Philippines.[58] China was his real target, but Korea came first, as offering the best invasion route. The Philippines were an afterthought, included chiefly because Hideyoshi had received a report that the small Spanish garrison would be a pushover. (The report was apparently correct. Most military historians agree that if Hideyoshi had reversed his order of attack, Manila would have been a Japanese city from 1592 on.)

During a campaign as Napoleonic as this, one might have expected the efficiency of guns to triumph over the mere heroism of swords and spears. It almost did. The Japanese started off to Korea with mixed upper- and lower-class units, their weapons as ill-assorted as ever. The samurai, who were a majority in nearly all detachments, carried their traditional two swords, plus at least one other weapon, usually either a bow or a spear. Most of the other soldiers carried guns. Of the original invading army of 160,000, somewhat over a quarter were matchlock-men.*

* This being a feudal army, with each territorial lord responsible for

During the first few months, while the Japanese were advancing up Korea almost at will, the diverse mixture of weapons worked well enough. The Korean army was so disorganized that the invaders could almost have fought with stone hatchets and won. As it was, they triumphed. The samurai fought with sword and spear against the Korean knights, routing them time after time. The lower-class gunners mopped up the remnants. It took the lead detachments just eighteen days from the first landing at Pusan until they captured Seoul. There was no danger of any Japanese being mopped up by Korean matchlockmen, because the Koreans had no matchlocks.

What the Koreans did have was a rather inefficient form of light artillery, which they had learned about from the Chinese. This the Japanese gunners outshot with no trouble at all, meanwhile devastating the Korean archers. It was an ideal war. Upper-class soldiers could be, and were, heroes; lower-class soldiers easily triumphed through technological superiority. They took particular pleasure in capturing the little Korean cannon, and General Kato Kiyomasa sent them home by the dozen as souvenirs. They are just over two feet long, and at infrequent inter-

equipping and clothing his own troops, there was naturally no set proportion of weapons. Some of the wealthier *daimyo* from central Japan had a good 40 percent of their men equipped with guns. Others, who like the Earl of Argyll were comparative backwoodsmen, brought practically no gunners at all.

Lord Tachibana Munishige, for example, sailed to Korea with 2,600 men. Two hundred of them were armored knights on horseback. Another 1,700 were dismounted samurai, most of them carrying long, glittering spears. Finally, he had 350 matchlockmen, and a mere 90 archers. Lord Shimazu Yoshihoro, on the other hand, commanding for his brother the Prince of Satsuma, brought about the same number of mounted knights, well over a thousand gunners, and practically no spearmen at all.[59]

Quartermaster supply in a sixteenth-century Japanese army must have been complicated.

A Japanese Cannon of Lord Oda's Time.
*This is a swivel breech-loading gun of light caliber, made in
Japan. By sixteenth-century standards, it fired quickly. In
Europe cannon of this sort were mounted as bow and stern
chasers on warships. In Japan they were mounted in castles as
well. The two light cannon placed in boats and used by Lord
Arima to rake the infantry columns of Lord Ryozoji's army as
they marched down the beach in 1584 were probably of this
kind.*

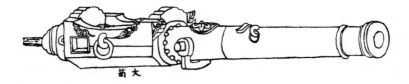

大筒

vals, fire a sort of large marble.[60] Useful for scaring Highlanders, but worthless against sixteenth-century Japanese.

But when the Chinese began to send whole armies of reinforcements to help the Koreans, the holiday atmosphere evaporated. Especially since in the second year of the war a few Korean units began to appear with matchlocks of their own. These were Korean-made – copied by smiths in northern Korea from the handful of captured Japanese weapons.* They were perfectly capable of killing a samurai.

The Japanese were now heavily outnumbered, and beginning to face serious resistance. The idea of guns for the whole army began to look very attractive to some of the commanders. A couple of letters written home from Korea in the 1590s reveal their view rather clearly. One was written in 1592 by a provincial lord who had gone over with approximately 1,500 archers, 1,500 gunners, and 300 spearmen. He wanted to change the ratio. 'Please arrange to send us guns and ammunition,' he wrote to his steward. 'There is absolutely no need for spears.'[62]

Seventeen years had passed since Nagashino, and it can hardly have been news to the steward that guns outperformed spears. The news was the change in his master's attitude. Incidentally, there were still plenty of guns in Japan to send. Francesco Carletti, the Florentine merchant, made his visit to Japan at the height of the Korean war, arriving from the Philippines in a

---

* Korea, which was at a considerably lower state of technology than Japan, did not get into serious gun production until the twentieth century. But its army recognized from 1592 on that the matchlock was a fine killing device. The first Korean gun manual, published shortly after the war, says, 'There are no guns like these in China; we got them from the Japanese barbarians. They are different from all other kinds of firearms. The good ones will go through armor. If you shoot a person, it hits his lungs. One can even hit the hole of a coin, not only just the willow leaf at 500 feet. . . . Either from a horse or on foot, a gun is more than ten times better than a spear, and five times better than a bow and arrow.'[61]

Japanese ship in 1597. Even though, as he later reported to Grand Duke Ferdinand de Medici, the Japanese now had nearly 300,000 men committed in Korea, there were still numerous samurai left at home. Most of them owned a gun or two, as he found when he got invited to go hunting. However much they might prefer sword and bow on the battlefield, for shooting ducks, pheasants, and wild geese, they liked guns. 'They kill all these with the arquebus, getting each with a single ball,' he wrote Duke Ferdinand.[63]

The other letter was written much later in the campaign, when the Japanese – rather like the Americans three hundred and fifty years later – had swept up to the Yalu River and then been driven down again by the Chinese (who made up a quarter of the world's population then, too). A Japanese nobleman named Asano was holding Yol-San Castle against a very much larger force of Koreans and Chinese, and he wrote his father to arrange for replacements. 'Have them bring as many guns as possible, for no other equipment is needed,' he said. 'Give strict orders that all the men, even the samurai, carry guns.'[64] In other words, the knightly retainers of the Asano family were to be dragged, kicking and screaming, into the late sixteenth century.

FOUR

Leaving out Hideyoshi's civilian-disarmament act, Japan seems at this moment – the winter of 1597 – to have been in much the same position as any European country, even to the views of its upper class. (Though in Europe the backlash against firearms began earlier, since firearms themselves arrived earlier.) For the Japanese were by no means alone in discovering that progress in weapons (a) meant more and faster killing, and (b) diminished human stature.

In France, Blaise de Montluc and the Chevalier Bayard despised firearms as much as any samurai did. Some Italian leaders, such as General Gian Paolo Vitelli, despised them even more. Vitelli felt so strongly the disgrace of having skilled swordsmen in his army shot from a safe distance by technicians with guns that after his successful siege of Buti, he cut off the hands of every arquebusier in the place.[65] That changed nothing. France and Italy went steadily on to the repeating rifle, while fifty years after Lord Asano's time the matchlock was getting rare again in Japan.

'Cannon and firearms are cruel and damnable machines; I believe them to have been the direct suggestion of the devil,' said Martin Luther.[66] But Germany moved ahead to become one of the great cannon foundries of Europe, while Japan continued making suits of armor far into the nineteenth century.

And in the very year that Lord Asano was writing home for more guns, Shakespeare was describing a young English lord who had chosen to give up a military career altogether, because firearms made war too ugly to contemplate. ('But for these vile guns,/ He would himself have been a soldier.' *Henry IV*, *Part One*, I, iii, 63–64.) Yet look ahead a couple of centuries, and you find the English systematically killing Chinese with guns far viler than any Shakespeare knew, and the Japanese having a prolonged renaissance of the bow and arrow.

There seem to be at least five reasons that explain why Japan, once she had made peace in Korea, could and did turn away from firearms, while Europe went rapidly ahead with their development. One – the most obvious – is that for every Blaise de Montluc there were a dozen samurai who felt that firearms were getting out of hand. The warrior class in Japan was very much larger than in any European country, amounting to somewhere between 7 and 10 percent of the entire population. No one knows exactly how large it was, because, though the Japanese government began taking censuses as early as 1590, the samurai were exempted from a procedure so demeaning as a headcount. The census simply omitted them. When they were finally counted, in the late nineteenth century, at the very end of the feudal period in Japan, there turned out to be 1,282,000 members of high samurai families (allowed to ride horses), and 492,000 members of low samurai families (entitled to wear two swords, but no horseback riding).[67] Since the non-samurai population remained quite stable during the entire period from the first census to about 1870, it seems reasonable to assume that the samurai population did, too. One would thus number the warrior class that winter of 1597 at nearly two million people – just under 8 percent of the population.

In England, by contrast, the warrior class in 1597 numbered

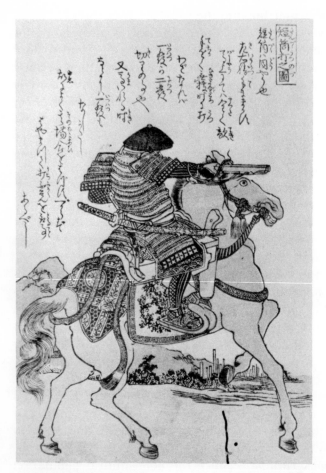

A Samurai Firearm.
*These pistols were designed for use on horseback – and hence
were to be fired only by members of upper samurai families.
'Don't waste your shots,' the Japanese caption warns aristocratic
shooters, 'because only one or two are available at a time.'
(From the* Budo Geijutsu hiden zue, *S. Yoshioka Collection,
Kyoto.)*

about 30,000 people. England had sixty lords, five hundred knights, and some 5,800 squires and gentlemen.[68] Together with their families, they made up six-tenths of a percent of the population. In no European country did the warrior class much exceed one percent.

A second reason is geopolitical. The Japanese were such formidable fighters, and islands are by nature so hard to invade, that territorial integrity could be maintained even with conventional weapons. Japan was much too small to conquer China – and when Lord Hideyoshi died in 1598, she quickly gave up the attempt – but much too fierce for anyone else to conquer *her*. The Portuguese never even considered trying; and though the thought seems to have passed through Spanish minds, it was quickly thrust out again. A Spanish royal decree of 1609 specifically directed Spanish commanders in the Pacific 'not to risk the reputation of our arms and state' against Japanese soldiers.[69] There was one engagement between Spaniards and some Japanese irregulars (mostly exiled samurai of the kind called *ronin*) in Siam in the 1620s, and it was the Spanish who lost.[70] As for the Chinese, though they won a number of battles during the Korean war, they were clear they could never have won the war itself. That war occurred, from their point of view, during the Ming Dynasty; and the official dynastic history summarizes the fighting in these words:

'The invasion by the Kampaku [Lord Hideyoshi] lasted nearly seven years. Casualties in the war exceeded many hundred thousand. . . . Though Korea and China fought hand in hand, they had no chance of victory. Only the death of the Kampaku brought the calamities of warfare to an end.'

And then the Chinese historian adds that right to the end of the dynasty – and the Mings ruled until 1644 – the memory of those fierce invaders stayed vivid. 'At the very mention of the Japanese, the people in the street became so excited that women and children held their breath in alarm.'[71]

A third and rather curious reason is that in Japan swords had a symbolic value far greater than they had in Europe. It would therefore have been a greater loss to let them be replaced entirely by guns.

To begin with, the sword was not merely a fighting weapon in Japan, it was the visible form of one's honor – 'the soul of the samurai,' in the Japanese phrase. So it was in Europe, too: a tap on the shoulder with a sword by the right person, and one arose a knight. But in Japan it was the *only* embodiment of honor – or, at least, the only one that formed part of one's costume. For a thousand years, Japanese men of the upper class wore no signet rings engraved with their coats of arms (or any rings at all), no jewels, no Order of the Golden Fleece, no military decorations, no gold epaulets. All that was concentrated into the beautifully worked handles and guards of the swords they fought with.

Or, again, swords stood for social importance far more than in feudal Europe. You couldn't even have a family name unless you also had the right to wear a sword. Peasants and merchants in feudal Japan lacked both. Occasionally a commoner would rise in the world and be granted a sort of life peerage. This was called *myoji-taito*, the privilege of surname and sword.[72]

Or, again, regular fighting swords doubled as major works of art. Almost four hundred years ago, Hideyoshi, as regent, appointed a man named Honami Kosetsu as the first of what has been an unbroken line of sword classifiers. The Japanese Ministry of Education continues in the 1970s to employ officials to examine and register samurai swords.[73] They can be registered in three classes of ascending dignity: important art objects, important cultural properties, and national treasures.

Swords are valued as works of art all over the world, of course, but not with the intensity that the Japanese value them. Probably only in Japan could an incident such as this in a battle in 1582 have occurred. General Hori Hidemasa was besieging Lord

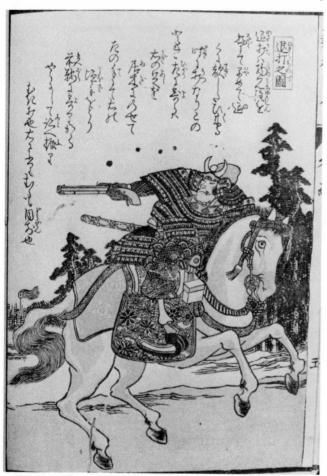

Shooting While You Retreat.
This print shows a special technique for shooting at enemies behind you. 'Lean well over to the left,' the caption says. 'Take your right foot out of the stirrup and prop it on top. Now turn your head and aim back over the horse's rump.' (S. Yoshioka Collection, Kyoto.)

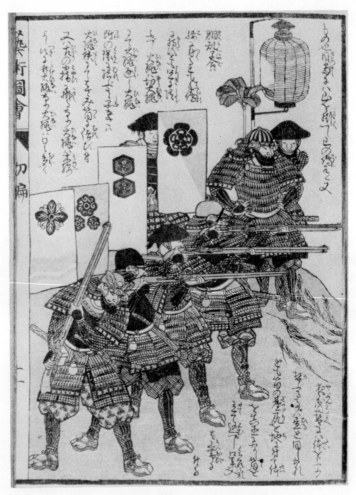

A Commander Trains Troops in Night Firing.
These are again gentlemen musketeers, as may be seen by the
two swords each man wears, and by the coats of arms in back.
Notice the Japanese lantern at the top. (S. Yoshioka Collection,
Kyoto.)

38

Akechi Mitsuhide in his castle of Sakamoto, and this was no siege half in sport, but a fight to the death.

Near the end, Lord Akechi sent out this message: 'My castle is burning, and soon I shall die. I have many excellent swords which I have treasured all my life, and am loath to have destroyed with me. . . . I will die happy, if you will stop your attack for a short while, so that I can have the swords sent out and presented to you.'[74] General Hori agreed, and fighting ceased while the swords were lowered out of the smoldering castle, wrapped in a mattress. Then it resumed, and the next day the castle fell and Lord Akechi died – presumably happy.

Furthermore, the sword remains to this day a source of metaphor in Japan for human characteristics. As the anthropologist Ruth Benedict has pointed out, the Japanese still speak of self-indulgent behavior as *'the rust of my body* – that figure of speech which identified one's body with a sword.'[75]

But the truly striking cases are those where swords and guns come up against each other. Two examples will suffice. The first took place in 1575. After Nagashino, one of the leading heroes of the battle – a young man of twenty-four who had held a small fortress principally with matchlockmen – received from his feudal superior a cascade of rewards. These included an increase in precedence, a wife, a landed estate, and a weapon appropriate to his heroism. It was no super-matchlock, but a Nagamitsu sword that had once been owned by a shogun.[76]

Thirty years later, when the government wanted to honor the four leading gunsmiths in Japan, it gave each of *them* a sword.[77]

Such symbolism exists in the West, too – it was a jeweled sword and not a jeweled burp gun that General Eisenhower received from the Queen of the Netherlands in 1947. But for several centuries the West has made a clear distinction between the merely nice and the actually useful. Or perhaps it would be better to say between what it admires and what it thinks works.

How to Shoot Accurately at Night.
*Infrared scopes did not exist in feudal Japan, but a technique
for shooting in the dark did. You tied a firing string (*hinawa*)
to your belt, which kept the gun at a fixed angle to your body.
Once you had zeroed in on a target, you could go on reloading
and firing, confident that your gun was at the right elevation.
(S. Yoshioka Collection, Kyoto.)*

John Nef, who has made a study of this split as it pertains to weapons, dates the final parting of the ways to the early seventeenth century.[78] He gives most of the credit (or blame) to north European Protestants. Before 1600, he points out, European fortresses and warships and cannon were made with just as much an eye to beauty as to effectiveness. And they were as likely to be designed by professional artists, especially painters and sculptors, as by military engineers.

Even as late as 1670, the French sculptor Pierre Puget was given the job of designing a fleet of new warships being built for Louis XIV at Toulon. But by then the split was nearly complete, even in a country as conservative and aristocratic as France. Colbert, Louis's chief minister, personally sent orders to Puget to stop making the ships so beautiful, and especially to stop cramming them full of sculpture. 'In their present-day naval constructions,' Colbert wrote, 'the English and the Dutch have scarcely any ornament, and they have no arcades at all. All these large pieces of work only serve to make the vessels much heavier, and subject to fires. . . . The sieur Puget should reduce the ornaments on the sterns that remain to be executed, whether the ships are on the stocks or in the water.'[79]

The samurai of Japan were never willing to make this distinction between what is beautiful and what is useful – or, at least, not until they met Commodore Perry, and not all of them then. The young hero's Nagamitsu sword was intended for possible actual use in some later battle; it was not just to lock away in a trophy room.

Still another reason is that the de-emphasis of the gun took place as part of a general reaction against outside ideas – particularly Christianity and the Western attitude toward business. Christianity was illegal in Japan after 1616, and the country was closed to foreigners in 1636 principally to keep missionaries from slipping back in. As for businessmen, a seventeenth-century shogun observed that 'merchants are fond of gain and given up to greed, and abominable fellows of this kind ought not to escape punishment.'[80]

In Europe, of course, guns were not an outside idea. Or if they were, no one realized it. As far as Europeans were concerned, they were something that had simply appeared long ago, back in the fourteenth or maybe the thirteenth century. The devil may have inspired them, but he was whispering in some European's ear when he did.

The fifth reason is the most curious of all. It is purely aesthetic. The symbolic value that swords had in Japan was more or less independent of how one physically handled them in battle. The symbolism could be attached to almost any weapon. It was, for example, to Colt revolvers in the American west. Men felt undressed and almost unsexed without them. ('If you ain't got a gun, why ain't you got a gun?' sneers a character in Stephen Crane's 'The Bride Comes to Yellow Sky.') Symbolic honor has been attached to spears at various times in Africa, and quite possibly it was to throwing sticks by cavemen.

Quite apart from all that, swords happen to be associated with elegant body movement. A sword simply is a more graceful weapon to use than a gun, in any time or country. This is why an extended scene of swordplay can appear in a contemporary movie, and be a kind of danger-laden ballet, while a scene of extended gunplay comes out as raw violence.

This much even an American recognizes. But for the Japanese there was an additional element. In Japanese aesthetic theory, there are some fairly precise rules about how a person of breeding should move his body: how he should stand or sit or kneel. In general it is desirable that he should have his knees together, and, when possible, his hands – the so-called concentration of body, will, and power. Furthermore, it is better if his elbows are not out at awkward angles. In some Japanese circles these rules still apply in the 1970s, in such ritual occasions as the tea ceremony.

A man using a sword, especially a Japanese two-handed *katana*, is naturally going to move his body in accordance with many of these rules. But a man firing an arquebus is not. He is going to break them.

There is in the New York Public Library a copy of a very beautiful Japanese manuscript which was once the private gun manual of a samurai named Kawakami Mosuke.[81] He had it made in 1595, at the height of the demand for guns during Lord Hideyoshi's Korean war. The copy in New York was done in 1607.

The manual consists of thirty-two pictures, showing all the positions from which one might fire a matchlock. Accompanying each picture there is written commentary by the experts of the Inatomi Gunnery School.[82] Mostly this is what you would expect in any gun manual. For example, one of the instructions to go with Number 9, a sitting position, reads, 'Take a deep breath and hold it.'

But some of the comments are quite different. Position 3, for example, which shows a man kneeling with the barrel of his matchlock resting on a stone, is accompanied by a series of almost apologetic remarks. First the writer apologizes for the stone. 'Soldiers used to have strong wrists and arms from swordplay. Now they must get in such awkward kneeling positions to shoot guns; their elbows hurt. Hips get a strange muscle pain.' And secondly he reminds the novice shooter of *bushi* rank that it's no good considering aesthetics. He must violate his principles if he wants to shoot accurately. '*Must* separate knees to kneel and fire.'

Even with guns, to be sure, the Japanese tried to preserve as much grace as they could. One of the instructions for Number 4, another kneeling position, reads, 'Keep seven inches between big

The Inatomi Gun Manual of 1595.
Here are seven of the 32 shooting positions taught by the Inatomi School of Gunnery. The figures are undressed not because the Japanese really shot (much less rode horses) that way, but so that a student using the manual could see exactly what position his arms and legs should be in. (From Japanese Ms. 53, Spencer Collection, The New York Public Library.)

toes as you kneel. One more inch does not look good.' The In-atomi School had once taught swordsmanship, and its teachers could not wholly forget old ways.

But in general the manuscript teaches mere ugly efficiency, and it apologizes for doing so. It also shows a good many signs of class consciousness. Even though it was written for a samurai, the illustrations all show a man with a peasant's haircut and wearing a peasant's breechclout (*fundoshi*) – as if it would be too much to show a gentleman in such ungainly postures. Even the calligraphy is ruder and coarser than was normal in man-uals of swordsmanship.

Maybe during a major war one would submit to these indig-nities, but once it was over, one reverted to good taste. Certainly most samurai did after 1600.

FIVE

There never was any formal abolition of firearms in Japan. In-stead, there was an extremely slow series of cutbacks, with no one point at which one might say: At this moment the Japanese gave up guns. In 1603, the first Tokugawa shogun – the *Britan-*

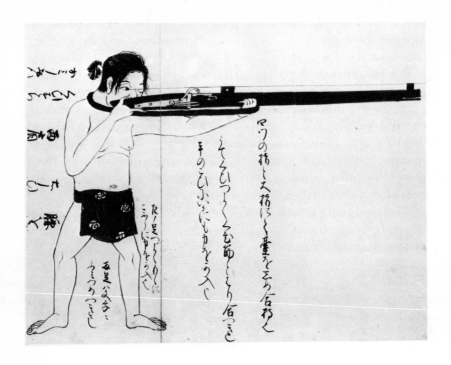

Inatomi Gun Manual.
Note the use of a gun sling. In sixteenth-century Japan this was called 'using the rope.'

nica's 'Jejessama' – took office, having conclusively established his primacy among the feudal lords at the Battle of Sekigahara, in 1600. Lord Tokugawa Ieyasu was approximately as powerful as his contemporary King James I of England – with whom, incidentally, he had a brief correspondence. That is to say, he could hand down edicts on a very broad scale, but if they were unpopular he could by no means always get them obeyed. Both rulers, for example, disapproved of smoking, and both ordered their subjects to give up the habit on pain of severe penalties; neither made the faintest impression. (One should perhaps add that while King James's objection was principally moral, Lord Ieyasu's was wholly practical. Because of the earthquake problem, most Japanese buildings were made of wood; and the habit of smoking in bed was causing an inordinate number of fires.)[83]

The matter of guns was handled differently. In Ieyasu's time, there were two great gun-manufacturing centers in Japan – one at Nagahama and one at Sakai, just south of Osaka. In addition, there was an unknown number of gunsmiths and powder-makers scattered through Japan, working for local rulers. Rear Admiral Arima Seiho, a retired Japanese naval officer of the Second World War, who has made an intensive study of firearms in the Far East, lists sixteen other places in Japan where guns were made between 1601 and 1604, but he doesn't claim to have got them all. Cannon were cast only at Nagahama and Sakai. Nagahama produced most of them, such as the five eight-pounders and ten six-pounders ordered by Ieyasu (and delivered to him) in 1600. But a fair-sized cannon still exists, cast at Sakai in 1611, and neatly inscribed, 'Made by Shibatsuji Ryuemon.'[84]

The Tokugawa shoguns first began to assert control over arms production in 1607. They started by calling in the four senior gunsmiths at Nagahama and giving them their swords – thus, of course, promoting them to samurai – and by simultaneously issuing a set of orders governing the industry. One was that guns

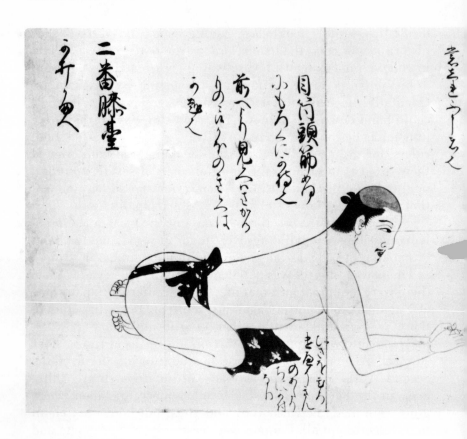

Inatomi Gun Manual.
Sighting in the gun.

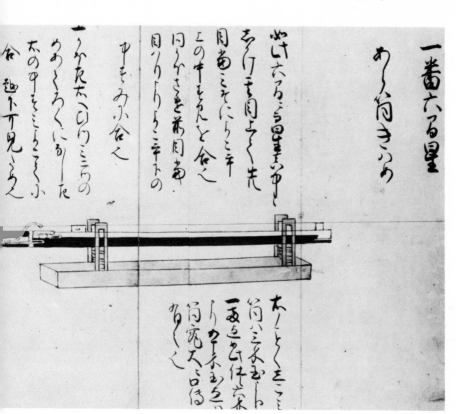

Inatomi Gun Manual.
The man guiding the boat (not visible in this picture) has offered to stop so that the man with a gun can get a better shot. 'That's not necessary,' the gunner answers. 'I know how to use the rhythm of the waves and aim flexibly.' In short, a self-confident Japanese marksman of the sixteenth century.

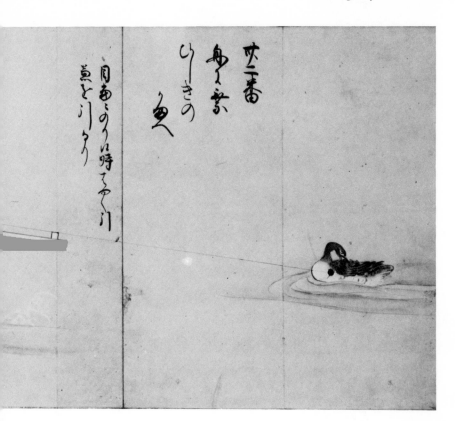

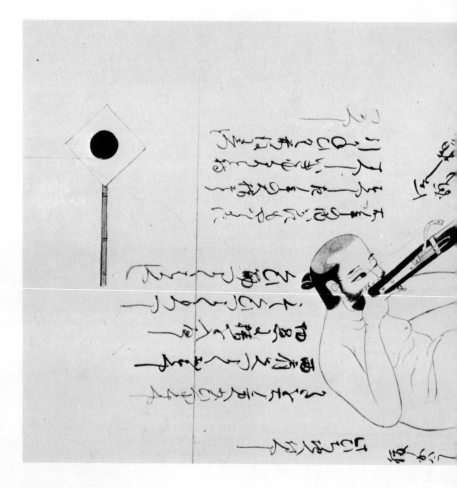

Inatomi Gun Manual.
High-angle fire. This was not a position the experts at Inatomi particularly recommended. It was hard to get an exact angle with your left leg. 'Sometimes when you fire,' the caption admits, 'the gun bounces off your foot.'

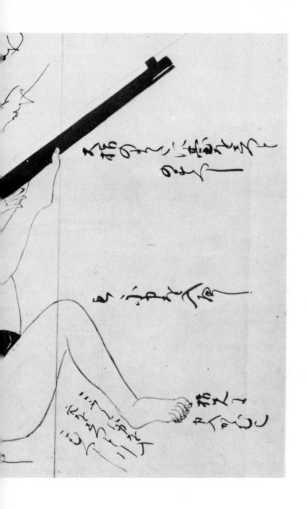

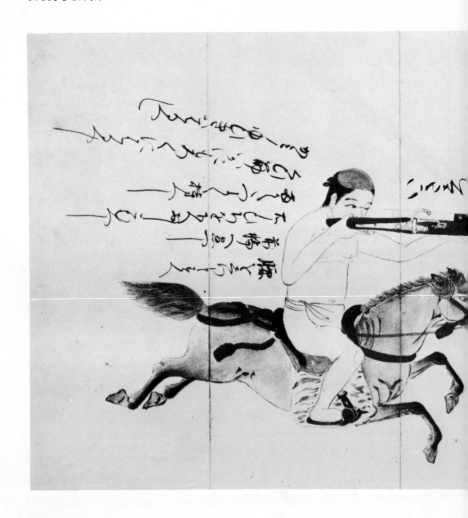

Inatomi Gun Manual.
'Grip tightly with both your knees,' the caption warns, 'when you shoot from a galloping horse.' The shoe-like stirrups also helped give stability.

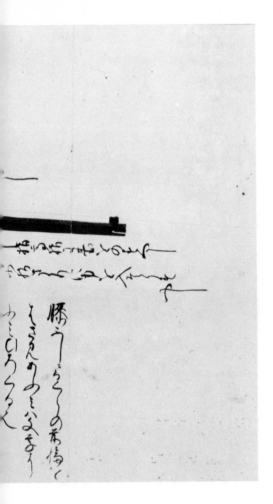

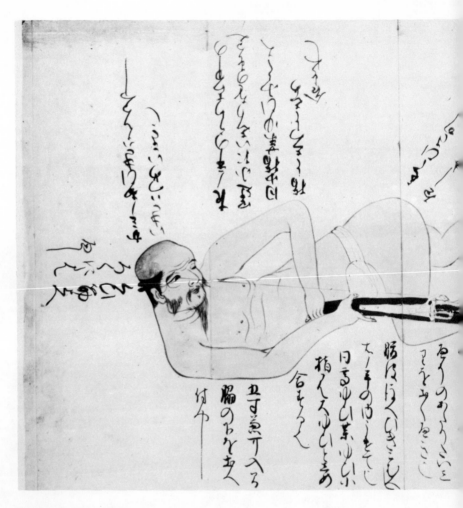

Inatomi Gun Manual.
This picture is pure show-off, a position for trick-shooters. (But there were Japanese gunners four hundred years ago who could do trick-shooting, just like Buffalo Bill or Annie Oakley.)

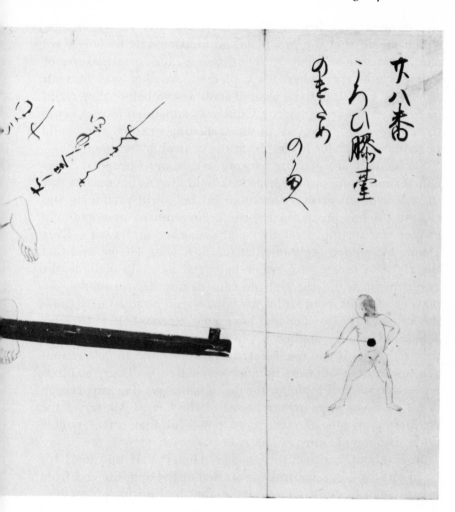

and powder were henceforth to be made only in Nagahama, which meant that the provincial gunmakers, one by one, were required to move there.[85] Swordmakers and spearmakers, of course, could stay where they pleased. Another was that all orders for guns had to be cleared with Tokyo before they could be filled. A Commissioner of Guns was appointed to make sure these rules were followed. In short, starting in 1607, guns could be made only under license from the central government.

Such edicts are nothing exceptional. Many European rulers issued similar ones as firearms took hold, just as in our own day the government of every country in the world producing nuclear arms has proclaimed them a government monopoly. In France, for example, another contemporary of Ieyasu's, King Henry IV, signed such an edict in 1601. King Henry said that the right to make gunpowder belonged as exclusively to the government as did the right to coin money. If you made gunpowder without a crown license, you would be fined fifty times the value of the powder and have your equipment confiscated. The same penalty applied if you had a license but made unauthorized sales. If you made not just powder but complete rounds of ammunition, you were in much worse trouble. Like a counterfeiter, you were eligible for the death penalty.[86] The supervision of all this was to be in the hands of the Grand Master of the Artillery – an official even more powerful than the Japanese Commissioner of Guns.

In England, considerably earlier, Henry VIII had tried his hand at actual gun control. He started at the opposite end from Ieyasu – not by limiting production, but by limiting ownership. An Act of Parliament of April 25, 1523 forbade anyone with an income of less than a hundred pounds a year to possess firearms, on pain of confiscation and a fine of forty shillings.[87] This meant that guns were lawful only for the upper gentry – as noted, a very small group indeed. In 1528 the King by proclamation changed the order to specify that an unauthorized gun was not to be confiscated but destroyed on the spot.[88] Another Act of Parliament, in 1533, increased the fine for illegal possession to ten pounds – that is, a year's wages for a master craftsman.[89]

But neither the French nor the English edicts were ever seriously enforced, because in neither country did enough people really dislike guns. The French edict was, in fact, unenforceable. Gunpowder was not made at a few large mills, but at scores and even hundreds of small mills all over France; and the government made no effort to consolidate them. Instead it attempted, not very vigorously, to license them all, and then purchase their whole output. In England, King Henry's desire to keep guns out of the hands of common people (who could and did use them to shoot deer illegally) was constantly coming into conflict with his even stronger desire to make England a leading military power. Right along, he had made an exception to the gun laws for all men living in fortified towns within seven miles of the coast, or of the Scottish border, 'for the only defense of the said Towns.'[90]

Furthermore, in 1543 he abruptly revoked the whole set of controls. He had declared war on France. Now he wanted 'his loving subjects practiced and exercised in the feat of shooting handguns and hackbuts* . . . for the annoyance of his majesty's enemies in time of war and hostility.'[91] By proclamation he authorized any male from the age of sixteen up to own and use a gun.

When peace came again, Henry revoked the revocation; and once more only the upper gentry (and men in walled towns within seven miles of the borders) could have firearms. But it was easier to send out the notice than it was to gather up the firearms again; and as for the skill in using them, Englishmen

---

* An English attempt to spell arquebus.

Scenes from a Seventeenth-Century Battle Screen.
The battle shown in this six-fold screen has not been identified;
the screen itself seems to have been painted about 1615. Note

the upper-class swordsmen fighting on horseback, and the lower-class gunners firing from behind breastworks and from the castle windows. (From the Kanamaru Collection, Japan.)

were no more going to lose that, just because peace was declared, than Americans were going to forget how to use in New York the modes of destruction they were taught in Vietnam. Furthermore, the ban didn't last. In 1557 there was another war, again with France. Again the gun laws were repealed.

Lord Tokugawa Ieyasu, however, really did centralize the production of guns and gunpowder, and he and his successors never went back on their policies. Not, anyway, until the reign of the fifteenth and last Tokugawa shogun, in the middle of the nineteenth century.

This is the way it happened. By the order of 1607, the gunsmiths of Japan had been assembled in Nagahama – all but those in Sakai. Ieyasu's power was not yet secure enough in 1607 for him to tackle Sakai. In theory, the Nagahama smiths were free to fill any orders they got, provided they had clearance from the Teppo Bugyo, or Commissioner of Guns. In practice, he cleared almost no orders except those from the central government. Since the central government was buying nothing except a few cannon, the provincial gunmakers soon began to starve. By 1608 they were slipping out of Nagahama again – going back to Choshu Province, or back to work for Lord Tokitaka's heirs on Tanegashima. In 1609 Ieyasu ordered them all back to Nagahama again, and this time he was prepared to offer a form of social security. The Teppo Bugyo was now authorized to give every gunsmith an annual salary whether he made any guns or not. All he had to do was stay in Nagahama, and let the government keep an eye on him.[92]

Even that didn't fully solve the problem. The salaries for not working were fairly low – and in any case the work ethic in Japan was (and is) strong. What most of the men wanted to do was work at their forges. Lacking orders for guns, a good many of them took up swordmaking. One of the two most famous swordsmiths Tokyo has ever produced, for example, started his career as a Nagahama gunmaker named Kiyotaka.[93] Then he changed his name to Hankei, moved to Tokyo — Edo it was then called — and began to make swords after the old style of Masamune.*

As for the ones who couldn't or wouldn't turn back to swords, in 1610 the government began to put in a dribble of orders. To make up for the small quantity, it paid what Admiral Arima describes as 'outrageously high' prices for each individual weapon.[95]

Things rocked along this way until 1625, by which time the government's monopoly was well established. A series of extremely gradual cutbacks then began. By 1673, the Japanese government had settled down to buying 53 large matchlocks one year, and 334 small ones the next. This annual order afforded a thin living to the four families of sword-wearing gunsmiths, and to about forty families of ordinary gunsmiths under them. In 1706, even the previous modest order was reduced. For the next eighty years, the production at Nagahama amounted to 35 large matchlocks in even years, and 250 small ones in odd years.[96] Considering that during all this time the number of samurai ran to half a million men or more, guns from Nagahama had ceased to be much of a factor in battle. (Or, since there virtually weren't battles after 1637, much of a factor in military training.) As a military weapon, they came to be used chiefly in ceremonial processions, as pikes are used at a modern British coronation.[97] Swords, spears, and bows, on the other hand, continued to be made in large numbers.

* Japanese swords are divided into *koto* or old swords, made before 1600, and *shinto* or new swords, made after 1600 — though since World War II, swords made between 1600 and 1700 have come to be known as *kinkoto* or near-old swords, and priced appropriately higher. The antique market is much the same everywhere. Hankei, the ex-gun manufacturer, not only learned to make swords, he made them *koto* style in the *shinto* period. One of his blades, still in Tokyo, was valued some years ago at $12,500.[94]

The manufacturers at Sakai were harder to bring under control at first. Unlike the provincial smiths, they were too numerous and too entrenched to be moved en masse to Nagahama, and they had powerful friends. Furthermore, Sakai had long been the nearest thing to a free city in Japan. The Jesuit missionaries went so far as to compare it with Venice, which with its complicated waterways it somewhat resembled physically as well as politically. For many years the manufacturers at Sakai could and did play off the Tokugawas in Tokyo against some of the semi-independent lords in other parts of Japan, and throughout the seventeenth century their business stayed fairly brisk.

In the early years of that century they were even able to export a few guns. A representative of the English East India Company, a man named Richard Wickham, was in Sakai in 1617, trying to put together a munitions order for Siam. The Governor of Sakai told him that gun export was completely illegal – but then suggested that he buy '3 or 4 at a tyme,' and he [the Governor] 'would not take notice thereof.'[98] In the end, Wickham was able to get twenty guns at the bargain rate of 1.2 taels. Some second-quality swords which were part of the same shipment cost 1.5 taels each. But twenty guns are barely noticeable compared to earlier export orders, such as those 87,000 swords to China. And within a few years, even tiny shipments like that ceased to leave Japan.

Domestically, Sakai did much better. The records still exist of their production between 1623 and 1690. It begins quietly with an average of two hundred and ninety matchlocks a year in the early 1620s, reaches a climax of twenty-five hundred a year in the 1660s, and then permanently dwindles off.[99] The central government never ordered a gun from Sakai after 1668, and Admiral Arima thinks that after 1696 no one else did, either. At any rate, over the next century the number of gunsmiths there gradually shrank to about fifteen, and this handful was supporting itself chiefly with government repair orders and by making iron farm tools.[100] They beat no swords into plowshares, but they unquestionably converted a few matchlocks.

.

Toward the middle of the seventeenth century, there was one last battle in Japan in which guns played a serious part. This was the Shimabara Rebellion in 1637. It was the last gasp of Christianity. It occurred twenty years after the expulsion of the missionaries and one year after the country had been closed to all Europeans except the handful of Dutchmen in Hirado, and a few remaining Portuguese traders, now confined to the tiny island in Nagasaki harbor.

There were still many Christian converts in the country, though, including several thousand landless samurai. These men had once been retainers of the half-dozen feudal lords who had become Christians, and who had since either gone back to Buddhism or lost their fiefs. In 1637 about 20,000 Christians in the old Portuguese sphere of influence in southern Japan joined a peasant rebellion – they were misled by a prophecy – and took over the castle of Hara. They had a fair number of guns, including five hundred and thirty they liberated from the armory of a local feudal lord, Matsukura Shigetsugu.[101]

After some delay, the government moved to put down the rebellion. In the ensuing battle, every single man in Hara Castle died except one, though not before killing many thousands of the besiegers. A song sung by the Christian rebels still survives. And while it does not sound very metrical in its English translation, it does give a vivid impression of both the constant gunnery and the extreme bloodthirstiness then typical of Japanese battles. The song goes like this:

> *While powder and shot remain,*
> *Continue to chase the besieging army*

Scene from a Seventeenth-Century Battle Screen.

That is blown away before us
Like the drifting sand.

Hear the dull thud of the enemy's guns: Don! Don!
Our arms give back the reply,
'By the blessing of God the Father,
I will cut off your heads!' [102]

But this was the last time the Japanese used guns with any readiness for over two hundred years. The samurai went back to taking fencing lessons, the monks resumed making black-feathered arrows, and all over Japan skilled smiths poured out a never-ending stream of top quality armor and swords. Just how small a role guns came to play can be gathered from a Japanese government document of 1725. That year a new king came to the throne in Korea. Since Japan and Korea had long since resumed friendly relations, the shogun sent him a ship-load of sumptuous coronation presents. Looking down the list, one finds 500 suits of heavy armor, 350 swords, 200 suits of light armor, 67 spears and halberds, and, finally, a pitiful 23 old-fashioned matchlocks. [103]

The new king's matchlocks could be nothing but old-fashioned, because research and development had also tapered off in Japan, coming to a dead stop long before 1725. Once one has learned to make matchlocks in large calibers, and once one has developed steel strong enough to prevent their barrels from bursting – which the Japanese did very quickly* – there is no-

---

* Early Japanese guns were astonishingly well made. Some of them were used in war for two or three generations in sixteenth and seventeenth century Japan. They were then retired to government storehouses for a couple of centuries – and then, when Japan resumed the active use of firearms after Commodore Perry, they were brought out and converted to percussion rifles for the new national army. They performed admirably. Still later, at the time of the Russo-Japanese war of 1904, some thousands of them were converted a second time, to bolt-action rifles. The American

where further to go, except on to flintlocks and, eventually, the neutron bomb. For two centuries the Japanese did not go further, although they knew about the next step at least as early as 1636, when the Dutch trading mission at Hirado presented the shogun with a dozen smart new flintlock pistols.[105] (It was one of their last efforts to avoid being moved to the little island at Nagasaki.)

A flintlock is not at all hard for a maker of matchlocks to copy. It would have been child's play for the smiths at Nagahama to set up a production line. But no one asked them to. Unlike Lord Tokitaka a century earlier, the shogun was simply not interested. The pistols went into a vault.

Nor was the shogun the only Japanese to know about flintlocks. A few years later, in 1643, a group of provincial samurai – 'Persons of Quality,' the seventeenth-century account calls them – were guests aboard the Dutch ship *Breskens*. The ship was full of technically advanced weapons. ('The Dutch are only good artillerymen, and beyond that fit for nothing save to be burnt as desperate heretics,' an early Portuguese historian, tired of Dutch pirates who attacked larger Portuguese ships, once wrote.)[106]

According to the custom of the time, the ship's cabin of the *Breskens* had half a dozen loaded flintlock muskets hanging on the walls. These the visitors idly examined, and 'out of curiosity, pulling the Tricker, they Fired.'[107] The ship's officers then spent about half an hour reloading the guns and passing them to the

gun expert Robert Kimbrough has written of these twice-retooled *tanegashima*: 'The author has seen bolt-action rifles which carried names and dates from the mid-1600s, and weapons so converted were for use with modern powder without blowing up! No higher praise can be given the workmanship of the old Japanese craftsmen.'[104]

Here, of course, is further proof that it was lack of interest rather than lack of ability that caused those old craftsmen to turn away from guns.

fascinated samurai, who blazed away so freely that the harbor-master came out to investigate. But no one offered a thousand taels, or even ten, for one of these rapid-fire weapons.

It's true that some governmental officials were still interested in heavy ordnance for coastal defence. As late as 1650, a Dutch gunner was in Tokyo for nine months, giving instruction in the casting of large cannon.[108] Records of what went on are extreme-ly scarce, and the Dutch gunner himself left no diary, but appar-ently the Japanese didn't really want to learn. It became an ac-cepted notion in Japan that eight-pounders were the largest cannon one could safely make, and it was eight-pounders – most of them two or three hundred years old – that were mounted as harbor defence in Tokyo Bay when Commodore Perry arrived in 1853. By then the Japanese had almost forgotten how to shoot them. One of the few intelligent foreigners to get a glimpse of Japan after 1650 was a Swedish botanist named Carl Peter Thunberg. He reported in 1776 that the coastal-defence guns were test-fired only once every seven years, and even then by means of a match on the end of a long pole. He also reported seeing an extraordinary number of very well made swords, which 'in strength and goodness surpass the manufactures of any other country.'[109]

The Dutch (even Thunberg was working for the Dutch trad-ing mission – it was the only way to visit Japan), the Dutch, of course, were puzzled by the persistent Japanese indifference to new weapons. They came up with a characteristically Dutch explanation. The reason, they decided, was 'neither dullness of perception . . . nor a prejudiced adherence to that to which they are accustomed, but a deficiency of flints in the geological for-mation of the country, and their determined aversion to depen-dence upon foreigners for anything essential to their military equipment.'[110] This was nonsense. There was and is plenty of flint in Japan.[111] Flint scrapers were used by the stone-age inhabitants of the country five thousand years ago. Flint lighters were used by Japanese aristocrats in the seventeenth century, when they smoked in bed. In fact, the European flintlock gun may have developed from those lighters.

No one is certain where or when the flintlock gun appeared. But in his classic *History of Firearms*, H. B. C. Pollard writes, 'There is also a possibility that the flintlock principle was brought back from Japan by Portuguese navigators, the Japanese having long used flint and steel mechanical lighters.' [112] To light their pipes, yes. But not to fire their guns. Why bother, if you don't want to use guns at all?

And not only did the Japanese not want to use guns, as the centuries went by they came to dislike even *seeing* them. In 1811 a Russian navy captain named Vassily Golovnin was taken prisoner in northern Japan, while exploring the Kurile Islands. He and six of his crew were held captive for two years. (Once again the well-educated Japanese got a shock at Western illiteracy. They could hardly believe it that not one of the four common seamen among the captives could even sign his name.) [113]

When the Russian Navy finally arranged their release in 1813, a warship was sent to Hakodate to pick them up. Its commander proposed to come on shore with a guard of honor consisting of two officers, two noncoms, and ten sailors carrying muskets. The local Japanese governor was adamantly opposed.

'We know of no instance,' he said, 'in which a foreign ambassador, whatever might be the object of his visit to Japan, has been permitted to present himself at a ceremonial conference with a retinue bearing firearms. Be satisfied with the same mark of respect which has been shown to other European ambassadors at Nagasaki; namely, that the men composing your suite shall be permitted to wear their swords, but let them leave their muskets behind them.' [114]

Captain Golovnin, incidentally, got a chance to look at the shore batteries at Hakodate. He said he felt he had been transported back to the time of Peter the Great. The emplacements were 'so foolishly constructed that it appears not only that they [the Japanese] understand nothing of the rules of the art, but that they are probably wholly deficient in experience.'[115]

And Golovnin did at least see actual if antique cannon. Sometimes there weren't even those. Thirty years after his release, an American whaling ship from Poughkeepsie, New York, ran aground and sank, not far from where he was captured. Its second mate, a young man named George Howe, and some sailors made it into the chief port of the island of Etorufu. That was on June 4, 1846. 'As we approached it, we saw what appeared to be a fort,' Howe wrote afterwards, 'but on coming nearer we found it was a piece of cloth extended about three-quarters of a mile, and painted so as to represent a fort with guns. Here, as we landed, about sixty men armed with swords and spears ran toward us.'[116]

Takeda Katsuyori and Lord Oda would scarcely have believed their eyes.

SIX

The rest of the story is soon told. Modern weapons did, of course, return to Japan. Even before Commodore Perry's fleet arrived, with its ten-inch naval guns and its iron sixty-four pounders,* a few Japanese had begun to press for renewed arms development. As early as 1809, stimulated by the intrusion into Nagasaki harbor of a heavily armed British frigate, a man named Sato Nobuhiro wrote and secretly published a book called *How to Use Three Types of Firearms*. In his eagerness to develop means of repelling further frigates, Sato also invented 'two types of miraculous bullets, which I called the New Thunder and the Golden-Purple Bell.'[118] In 1828, another modernizer finally took the hint that the Dutch trading mission had given in 1636, and began furiously experimenting with flintlock weapons. He used native flint. In 1852, the year before Perry's first visit, still a third modernist, this one named Sakuma Shozan, made a private inspection of ten shore batteries near Tokyo, all of which he found principally armed with six- and eight-pounders cast before 1620. The disposition of the guns, he said, 'made no sense, and none of them could be depended on as a defense fortification.' He added, 'I struck my chest, and wept for a long time.'[119]

But these men had almost no effect on the general preference for swords and bows. It was Commodore Perry who caused the reintroduction of firearms into Japan; he accomplished it by convincing the majority of the Japanese leaders that the only way to keep future Perrys out of Tokyo Bay was to get ten-inch naval guns of their own. Even then, the resistance was extraordinary. It culminated in 1876, nine years after the old feudal regime had toppled. The last Tokugawa shogun had resigned, the shogunate itself had been abolished, the three hundred feudal lords had been replaced by civil servants. Now the new government, anxious to get ahead faster with modern military

---

* So much bigger than the little guns on shore that, as one of Perry's officers boasted, he could have loaded his guns with entire Japanese cannon as projectiles, and fired them back at their owners. Just what Kato Kiyomasa's men presumably said about the tiny Korean cannon in 1592.[117]

methods and a national army, forbade the samurai to continue wearing their two swords.

For many samurai this was the last straw. On the night of October 24, 1876, a hundred and seventy of them, dressed in armor and carrying swords, attacked the national troops stationed at Kumamoto, killing about three hundred of them, including the major general in command.[120] That attack proved abortive, but it led to a full-scale rebellion the next year, in which something like 40,000 samurai took part. It required the entire national army, less one, to put them down. That one was Field Marshal Saigo, the commander-in-chief, who was not available to help defeat the Satsuma Rebellion because he had joined it.

An American teacher who was living in Japan in 1877 has left a description of the rebels, which would serve equally well for an account of Takeda Katsuyori's army in 1575. Most of them, he wrote, 'were equipped with the keen double-handed swords of feudal times, and with daggers and spears. It seemed to be their opinion that patrician samurai could rush into close quarters with the *heimin* [peasant soldiers] and easily rout them,' even though the *heimin* were equipped with rebuilt matchlocks and modern French rifles.[121] Lord Takeda could have told them otherwise. So could Lord Matsudaira, Warden of Kami Province, who said disgustedly of the 1637 rebellion. 'In this there is no difference between soldiers and peasants, because firearms are used.'[122]

The American teacher himself was less sure, since he recalled an incident a few years earlier in which two samurai had attacked twelve fully armed British dragoons in Kyoto (they were the embassy guard), and had disabled nine of them with spectacular swordplay, not getting a single bullet wound themselves.[123] But urban guerrilla warfare is a special case. A full-scale battle of guns against swords can have only one outcome, and the rebellion of 1877 substantially followed the course of

Noel Perrin

The Rebellion at Kumamoto.
*On October 24, 1876, 170 angry samurai gathered at Fujisaki
Shrine and formed an army called the Shinpuren. In this wood-
block print by Nagashima Mosai, government troops are shown*

74

battling one unit of the Shinpuren. What looks like a severed head in the center foreground actually belongs to a rebel who is carrying a wounded comrade on his shoulders and simultaneously looking back at the government cavalry.

Noel Perrin

Nagashino. Indeed, allowing for the fact that the firearms were
so much more modern in the Satsuma fighting, the two battle-
fields must have looked remarkably alike. During the main battle, which occurred on February 17th and 18th, 1878, there were
many single combats between armored samurai. (The government had hastily enlisted some northern samurai to combat the
rebels.)[124] No doubt some were preceded by introductions. But
even as their swords flashed, the air was thick with the 322,000
rounds of ammunition and the 1,000 artillery shells the government averaged each day.[125]

Another American living in Japan in the 1870s – a Boston sea
captain named John Hubbard – had a chance to examine the
battlefield the day after. Two things impressed him. One was
the stacks of captured rebel weapons, in which a few small arms,
chiefly non-rebuilt matchlocks, were totally overshadowed by
the number of captured swords, which rose in a mound 'at least
ten feet from the ground' and 'were of all sizes and lengths, and
appeared to have had some very rough usage.' The other was a
fortification in the rebel lines. 'Here, to our astonishment, we
found two wooden cannon. One was 8 ft. 6 in. long, with a 9 in.
bore, made of two hollow pieces of wood and hooped its entire
length with bamboo hoops. It . . . did not appear to have been
used, but was mounted in a pile of sandbags ready for use. A
smaller one, about 6 ft. long, was lying near and dismantled;
this had been fired and was badly burst.'[126] Shibatsuji Ryuemon
and his colleagues at Sakai would have been appalled at such
primitive weapons.

Ten years later they would have been amazed at the change.
From 1878 to the present, Japan's attitude toward firearms has
been much like that of any other developed industrial society.
The clock that had been turned back was turned forward again
with almost incredible speed. Before 1900, Japan had again
caught up militarily with the Western world. Viewed from the

nuclear present, her two hundred and fifty years of technological retrogression may seem to have no great significance, except as a historical curiosity, and perhaps as proof that a deliberate turning back is in fact possible in a civilized society.

But viewed firsthand by contemporaries, they were another matter. The most famous of such views is that of a European scientist, Engelbert Kaempfer, M.D., Ph.D., who managed to spend two years in Japan in the late seventeenth century, about two generations after guns had been renounced. (By serving with the Dutch trading mission, of course.) Dr. Kaempfer had grown up in a Europe that had used firearms so enthusiastically during those same two generations that the population of his native Germany had been cut in half. Land values in some regions were a twentieth of what they had been; cannibalism was fairly common; and in one German duchy – Franconia – grown men were so scarce that surviving Catholic priests were encouraged to marry, and other men to take two wives.[127]

In the final paragraph of his three-volume *History of Japan*, Dr. Kaempfer summarizes the strikingly different situation of the Japanese. 'United and peaceable, taught to give due worship to the Gods, due obedience to the Laws, due submission to their Superiors, due love and regard to their Neighbors; civil, obliging, virtuous, in art and industry exceeding all other nations, possessed of an excellent Country, enriched by mutual Trade and Commerce among themselves, courageous, abundantly provided with all the necessaries of life, and withal enjoying the fruits of peace and tranquillity. Such a train of prosperities must needs convince them, whether they reflect on their former loose way of life or consult the Histories of the remotest ages, that their Country was never in a happier condition that it now is.' [128]

A Swordfight in 1877.
*The Fighting Women's Army of Kagoshima – a group of women
of samurai families who had joined the Satsuma Rebellion – is
holding a bridge against cavalry of the newly formed national
army. Notice the men's weapons. Though the new government
had equipped its infantry with modern rifles, the cavalry still*

used spears. The women are fighting with naginata, *the ancient long-handled sword, and with regular samurai swords. Notice also the distinction in dress. The men have uniforms of nineteenth-century European design; the women are fighting in highly individualistic kimonos of traditional Japanese design. (Copyright by Bradley Smith. From* Japan: A History in Art.*)*

79

SEVEN

POSTSCRIPT

The idea of turning back the clock has, of course, occurred to men in the West many times. Bayard – who, like Lord Mori Nagayoshi, died of a bullet wound – would have been only too happy to. Queen Elizabeth I not only thought about it, she actually once did set the hands back a fraction of a second. A subject of hers named William Lee had invented a knitting machine, with which he hoped to replace hand-knitting as the universal method of making stockings in England. He succeeded in interesting the Queen's cousin, Lord Hunsden, in this early bit of automation. Lord Hunsden, in turn, tried to get Elizabeth both to grant Lee a patent and to invest crown funds in a prototype factory. She would do neither. 'My lord,' she said, 'I have too much love for my poor people who obtain their bread by knitting to give money to forward an invention which will tend to their ruin, by depriving them of employment.'[1] That was in 1589.

In our own time, Arnold Toynbee, among others, has wanted to put the clock back several hours. His argument is that men can no more be trusted not to abuse modern technology than a kindergarten class could be trusted to play with machine guns. 'If a vote could undo all the technological advances of the last three hundred years,' Toynbee has written, 'many of us would cast that vote, in order to safeguard the survival of the human race while we remain in our present state of social and moral backwardness.'[2]

Even some scientists, such as the biologist René Dubos, would like to see the clock of technology, if not turned back, then stopped more or less at its present moment. Dr. Dubos is moved less by fears that now we can all kill each other, we will, than by dismay at our reckless expenditure of natural resources. Unlike some others who are dismayed, he has predicted that by the year 2000 we will be driven by the needs of conservation into what he calls 'a phase of steady state,' technologically speaking.[3]

But the number of those who seriously hope to set back the clock, or even to stop it, remains very small. To most men who have considered the matter, there seem to be two overwhelming objections. First, ignoring (or unaware of) the Japanese experience, they suppose it is just not possible to reverse technology within a continuous culture. Second, if by some miracle (such as Toynbee's vote taking place, and God heeding it), it *were* possible, they think it would lead to decadence and stagnation. They see the choice as either continued progress in all fields, or else a return to the Dark Ages. Either we press on with neutron bombs and biogenetic engineering, or we give up dentistry and window glass. Selective control of technology is impossible, they suppose.

The history of Tokugawa Japan does not support this gloomy view, however. The Japanese did practice selective control. They utterly ceased weapons development – indeed, went backwards – and meanwhile they went ahead in dozens of other fields. Slowly, to be sure. Technological change occurred much more gradually in seventeenth, eighteenth, and early nineteenth century Japan than in the West. It may even have occurred at a rate better suited to the human mind. There was no future shock in

A New Age Begins.
*Soldiers of the shogun practice cannonry about 1860. It is hard
to tell from this woodcut, but probably both the cannon and the*

soldiers' guns are retooled seventeenth-century weapons. The bayonets, however, are brand-new. (Copyright by Bradley Smith. From Japan: A History in Art.*)*

Tokugawa Japan. But it did occur. Japan was neither decadent nor stagnant.[4] Obviously there were decadent elements and stagnant pockets – but there are in most societies at most times. Take the country as a whole, and one finds health and vitality.

For example, in the seventeenth century, at the very time that guns were phasing out, waterworks engineering had its real beginning in Japan. Tokyo began to be supplied by aqueduct in the 1640s, as its population neared half a million. The second and principal Tokyo aqueduct, completed in 1654, ran some twenty-five miles. New York's first aqueduct was slightly longer – about thirty-three miles – but it was not built until 1842.[5] In 1654, New York City got its water from a well operated by a hand pump.

Nor were the two Tokyo aqueducts some kind of special case, reflecting not so much advances in technology as the great wealth of the Tokugawa shoguns and their love for their new capital city. Because at that same moment in Japanese history, large-scale irrigation canals began to appear all over the country. Japan being so mountainous, sections of most of them had to be tunneled through solid rock. Such canals were considerable engineering works. The Kasai Canal, one of the earliest, went into operation in 1660, just about the time the last cannon was cast for two hundred years. It was forty miles long, and supplied water to something over 20,000 acres of rice paddy.[6]

Or consider metallurgy and mining. The Japanese had been renowned metalworkers for several hundred years before Lord Ieyasu took control of the country. With cannon gone and the production of small arms declining, with the export market in armor and swords wholly closed, with the country at utter peace from 1637 on, and almost no defense budget to rely on, with so high a technical level to fall from, one might look for a touch of decadence here. Not at all. There was development. For example, in 1697 water-powered crushing mills began to be used in the smelting of gold and silver.[7] About the same time, a new blower (*tenbin-fuigo*) was developed for use in iron-smelting.[8] And the first technical book on mining was published: Kurosawa Motoshige's *Kozan Shiho Yoroku*, 1691.[9] In the next century, gunpowder began to be used to blast the ore free in deep mining. War was not needed to produce all this.

Neither was foreign contact needed to produce advances in more theoretical fields. Take mathematics. As every mathematician knows, that field was dominated in the seventeenth century by two towering figures: Sir Isaac Newton and Gottfried von Leibnitz. One Englishman and one German, contemporaries. Newton lived from 1642 to 1727, Leibnitz from 1646 to 1716. Each, working independently, claimed to have discovered calculus.

What very few mathematicians know is that there was a third figure of equal eminence alive at the same time. He was, in fact, born in the same year as Newton. Seki Takakazu was the great exponent of a purely Japanese type of mathematics called *wasan*. It owed nothing to Europe. He was as unaware of Newton and Leibnitz as they were of him. This did not stop him from finding a *wasan* method for solving cubic equations, or from dealing with negative and imaginary roots – or even from introducing the concept of the matrix in 1686, well ahead of Leibnitz's separate introduction of it to Europe.[10] Nor was Seki alone. His successors, distinguished mathematicians like Araki, Matsunaga, Yasujima, and Uchida, continued to develop *wasan* for the next two hundred years. (The Japanese, it should be added, are just generally good at math. They switched from *wasan* to Western math after Perry, and continue to shine. Edwin Reischauer, writing in 1977 of Japanese education, says, 'General levels of educational achievement are usually not susceptible to measurement across language barriers, but where they are, as in the field of mathematics, the Japanese have tended to rank first in the world.')[11]

As for agriculture, progress of many sorts occurred throughout the Tokugawa period. The two-bladed plow called the *nichogake* was introduced, the spiked-wheel potato planter, and the *kusakezuri* weeding machine.[12] And the results of such new machinery and of steady crop research showed everywhere. Silk production doubled between 1600 and 1700 and then quadrupled between 1700 and 1800.[13] The number of varieties of rice increased from 175 in 1600 to about two thousand in 1850.[14]

There were no such developments in every field, and Japan certainly did not – until after the fall of the Tokugawa shogunate in 1867 – go through an industrial revolution. The changes I have been describing took place slowly and, on the whole, painlessly, which by definition is not the case in an industrial revolution. But within the relatively stable economy and culture of that long tranquil period, changes of almost any sort remained possible. To give an example very different from any of the preceding, mail service improved spectacularly during the eighteenth century in Japan. There were armored knights striding around Tokyo and Kagoshima when the Continental Congress was meeting in Philadelphia – but a letter, or a shipment of lacquer tree seedlings, traveled many times faster between those two cities than mail did between Philadelphia and Savannah.[15]

Then there is medicine. Though Japanese medicine was unquestionably inferior to Western, it did make advances throughout the period. In the eighteenth century a few Japanese doctors even took up the study of anatomy; in 1754 one of them published the first local anatomy text, called *Zoshi* (or, *On the Internal Organs*).[16] More striking, in 1805 a surgeon named Hanaoka Seishu performed an operation using the new Japanese anesthetic *mafutsusan*. Ether had not yet come in in the West, and this is generally held to be the first surgical operation in the world performed under general anesthesia.[17] It is true that within a mile or two of the hospital one could have found feudal soldiers practicing with the bow and arrow.

One final example of Tokugawa progress, this from the field of retail merchandising. In 1813, Vassily Golovnin, the Russian navy captain mentioned earlier, had a chance to visit several Japanese stores. This was in a minor provincial city in the far north of Japan.

What he found on the counters he could not have found in his homeland or in the United States for many years to come. That is, row after row of prepackaged and prepriced goods. Captain Golovnin was very impressed to see that practically all of the things for sale bore 'little printed bills, on which are noted the price, the use, and the name of the article, the name of the maker or factory, and often something in their praise.' Point-of-purchase advertising, in fact. 'Even tobacco, pomatum, tooth-powder and other trifles,' he went on, 'are wrapped up in papers on which a notice of the quality and price is printed.'[18] In an American store in 1813, there would have been cracker barrels, pickle barrels, bolt goods, and so forth, but there would not have been modern packaging or pricing techniques.

But the vitality of Tokugawa Japan perhaps appears most clearly in the testimony of the first generation of foreigners to visit the country after Perry reopened it. Such Westerners as the Boston scientist Edward Morse and the British diplomat Sir Rutherford Alcock on the whole expected to find a backward land – and they didn't, any more than Don Rodrigo Vivero y Velasco had in 1610.

Professor Morse, for example, found himself 'astonished at learning the death-rate of Tokyo was lower than that of Boston.'[19] New York, too. In New York, Typhoid Mary was still to come. In Tokyo, diseases like typhoid were wholly absent. When

Noel Perrin

The Nineteenth-Century Through Japanese Eyes.
*This is not a scene from the Middle Ages but from the period
1815-1820. It is an illustration taken from a contemporary
Japanese life of Napoleon. He is shown in exile on St. Helena,*

guarded by four British soldiers. The actual British troops on St. Helena did not, of course, wear armor or carry swords and spears.

Morse investigated to find why, it turned out to be because the Japanese were so far ahead in sanitary engineering. He was almost equally startled when he took a sixty-mile cross-country trip to Nikko, and found himself on 'a much better road than ever I saw in New England, outside the cities.'[20] Funny little Orientals with swords weren't supposed to have roads like that.

Other visitors recorded their surprise at finding such things as operating oil wells at Echigo which had been brought in thirty years before the first American oil wells,[21] recycling so efficient that there was simply no debris to be found in Japan,[22] and a merchant marine (composed entirely of sailing ships between fifty and two hundred tons) larger than that of most Western countries.[23]

But let them use their own words. Here are five foreign judgments of Japan made just as the feudal age was ending and just before her incredibly rapid industrial revolution began. Japan was then a self-supporting and self-sufficient country of thirty million people, unpolluted, the product of two hundred years of existing in a phase of steady state, and very beautiful. She is none of these things, of course, in 1979.[24]

'I have heard everywhere the happy laughter of your children, and never been able to discern misery.' Henry Heusken, First Secretary of the American Legation, 1857.[25]

'The people all appeared clean, well fed . . . well clad and happy looking. It is more like the golden age of simplicity and honesty than I have ever seen in any other country.' Townsend Harris, U.S. Consul General, 1858.[26]

'[I saw] peace, plenty, apparent content, and a country more perfectly cultivated and kept, with more ornamental timber everywhere, than can be matched even in England.' Sir Rutherford Alcock, 1860.[27]

'It is not true that we resort to Japan to civilize, for civilization exists already; or to convert the heathen, for such attempts are strictly forbidden under the terms of the treaty which we have accepted; or to add to the happiness of the people, for a more contented people does not exist; or for any object in the world but to trade with profit to ourselves.' General Edward Barrington de Fonblanque, R.A., 1861.*[28]

'A foreigner, after remaining a few months in Japan, slowly begins to realize that, whereas he thought he could teach the Japanese everything, he finds to his amazement and chagrin, that those virtues or attributes which under the name of humanity are the burden of our moral teaching at home, the Japanese seem to have been born with.' Edward S. Morse, Professor of Zoology, Imperial University, Tokyo (and later president of the American Academy for the Advancement of Science), 1877.[30]

None of this proves in the least, to be sure, that what the Japanese once did with guns the whole world could now do with, say, plutonium. Japan's circumstances in the seventeenth century were utterly different from those of any military power now.

What the Japanese experience *does* prove is two things. First, that a no-growth economy is perfectly compatible with prosperous and civilized life. And second, that human beings are less the passive victims of their own knowledge and skills than most men in the West suppose. 'You can't stop progress,' people com-

---

* General de Fonblanque's own actions in Japan support his implication that Westerners could only corrupt. He was there buying cavalry horses for the British Army, which was then fighting in China. He bought several thousand, all stallions. This wasn't because he preferred stallions, but because castrated horses were not to be had. 'Gelding is considered a barbarous and cruel practice, and is not likely to be introduced,' he noted.[29]

Then he introduced a barbarous and cruel practice of his own. He had brought a branding iron with him from England. These stallions were now horses of the Queen; and, as they plunged and screamed, he had each one branded with the alien initials VR.

monly say. Or in a formulation scientists are especially fond of, 'What man can do, man will do.' Once he learns how to alter the DNA code, the theory goes, it is inevitable that he *will* alter it. Once the technology exists for supertankers, there is no going back to small tankers, much less sailing ships. If computers in the year 2001 are more efficient than men at doing most of the processes lumped together under the term 'thinking,' then computers will do most of the thinking.

This is to talk as if progress – however one defines that elusive concept – were something semidivine, an inexorable force outside human control. And, of course, it isn't. It is something we can guide, and direct, and even stop. Men can choose to remember; they can also choose to forget. As men did on Tanegashima.

NOTES

FOREWORD

1. Purists will object to this statement. The Japanese had been
   familiar with gunpowder for centuries, and they had encountered the primitive Chinese guns called *tetsuho* (literally, iron tubes) at least 270 years before Europeans
   arrived in Japan. There is some evidence that they possessed a few *tetsuho* of their own. If so, these simple
   weapons (no sights, no trigger) did not affect either warfare or the national consciousness. As S. R. Turnbull says
   in *The Samurai: A Military History*, 'The weapons
   brought by the Portuguese were undoubtedly the first
   real "firearms" that had ever reached their country.'
   (Turnbull, *Samurai*, p. 137.)
2. This belief eventually turned into a full-blown myth. Later
   Japanese accounts of the early Christian missions present
   them entirely in terms of *realpolitik*. One popular eighteenth-century version begins like this. (The 'Southern
   Barbarians' are the Portuguese and Spanish – who did
   in fact share kings between 1580 and 1640.)
   'One day the King of the Southern Barbarians said to
   his council: "I am told that far to the east lies a country

called Japan and that it abounds in gold, silver, and precious stones. Why should not that land be subjugated and added to my domains?" '

But one of his generals answers that this is impossible – by open invasion. 'The Japanese are too brave warriors to be overcome by force of arms,' he says. 'In my opinion, the best way to make ourselves masters of the land is by means of our religion.' Convert a third of the people, the general advises, and *then* send the army. (Otis Cary, *A History of Christianity in Japan*, p. 243.)

3. An example which has been famous for two hundred years is the ignorance of a Dutch merchant named Arend Willem Feith. Feith spent fourteen years on Deshima in the 1760s and 1770s, and during that time led five Dutch embassies to the shogunal court in Tokyo. It was to go on the annual embassy that Dutchmen were allowed on the mainland. At the end of the fourteen years, he had not even learned the name (Tokugawa Ieharu) of the shogun whose court he had five times visited. (C. R. Boxer, *Jan Compagnie in Japan*, pp. 139–140.)

MAIN TEXT

1. Quoted in Rudolph Flesch, *The New Book of Unusual Quotations* (New York: Harper & Row, 1966), p. 336.
2. Gardner, *The Case of the Turning Tide* (New York: William Morrow & Co., Inc., 1941), p. 36.
3. Lord Dunsany, *Patches of Sunlight* (London: Heinemann Ltd., 1938), p. 23.
4. Allan B. Cole, ed., *Yankee Surveyors in the Shogun's Seas*, p. 43.

5. See James Murdoch, *A History of Japan*, II, pp. 485 and 489–490; and Cary, *Christianity in Japan*, p. 161.
6. *Encyclopaedia Britannica*, 6th ed., IX, 37.
7. There is a whole literature on this incident. The earliest European account of it (in Fernao Mendes Pinto's *Peregrinacion*, written ca. 1558–1569, published 1614) is partly a fabrication, which has been gradually corrected over a period of more than three centuries. The fullest and most reliable account I have found – it attempts to reconcile all known European and Japanese sources – is in Seiho Arima's *Kaho no Kigen to Sono Denryu (The Origin of Firearms and Their Early Transmission)*, pp. 615–633.
8. Peter Pratt, *History of Japan, Compiled From Records of the English East India Company*, I, p. 265.
9. Margaret T. Hogden, *Change and History: A Study of the Dated Distribution of Technological Innovations in England*, pp. 181–182.
10. Delmer M. Brown, 'The Impact of Firearms on Japanese Warfare,' p. 238. See also Arima, *Kaho no Kigen to Sono Denryu*, p. 662. Lord Oda was sixteen at the time, newly come into his estate; and it seems to have been his gunnery instructor, a man named Hashimoto, who actually prompted the order.
11. Quoted in Louis-Frédéric, *Daily Life in Japan at the Time of the Samurai*, p. 173.
12. A. L. Sadler, *The Maker of Modern Japan*, p. 53. The general had been commanding the fortress of Marune, which was captured by Tokugawa Ieyasu on June 22, 1560, 'making good use of concentrated arquebus fire.' (Turnbull, *Samurai*, p. 144.) This was seventeen years after the arrival of guns.

13. Henry James Coleridge, *The Life and Letters of St. Francis Xavier*, II, p. 331. St. Francis honored Japanese swords himself. Visiting the lord of Bungo in 1551, 'Francis knelt to kiss his scimitar, a sign of great respect in Japan,' Coleridge, *St. Francis*, II, p. 315.

14. K. Glamann, 'The Dutch East India Company's Trade in Japanese Copper,' p. 59.

15. Carlo M. Cipolla, *Guns and Sails in the Early Phase of European Expansion, 1400–1700*, p. 51n.

16. Ibid., p. 35n.

17. Pratt, *History of Japan*, I, p. 22 .

18. Donald F. Lach, ed., *Asia on the Eve of Europe's Expansion*, p. 149.

19. Sir Richard Temple, ed., *The Travels of Peter Mundy*, III, Pt. I, pp. 294–295.

20. C. R. Boxer, *The Christian Century in Japan*, 1951, p. 68. Japan was capable of mass production nearly a thousand years before any European country was. The most striking example I know is the order placed by the Empress Shoken in the year 764 – for one million miniature wooden pagodas, each to contain four Buddhist incantations printed on a long strip of paper. The order, mass-produced on lathes, was completed in 770. The Empress gave 100,000 of the little pagodas to each of ten great monasteries. Most have vanished over the ensuing 1200 years – but the Horyuji monastery still has a large number. The Peabody Museum in Salem, Mass., has one. (See F. A. Turk, *The Prints of Japan*, p. 28; Money Hickman and Peter Fetchko, *Japan Day by Day: An Exhibition Honoring Edward Sylvester Morse*, pp. 56–57.)

21. Francesco Carletti, *My Voyage Around the World*, tr. Herbert Weinstock, p. 32.

22. Ludwig Riess, 'History of the English Factory at Hirado,' pp. 54–55.

23. Boxer, *Christian Century*, p. 68.
24. Arnoldus Montanus, *Atlas Japannensis*, p. 65.
25. George Cameron Stone, *A Glossary of the Construction, Decoration, and Use of Arms and Armor*, p. 318.
26. Inami Hakusui, *Nippon-To, the Japanese Sword*, p. 118.
27. Boxer, *Christian Century*, p. 62.
28. Donald F. Lach, *Asia in the Making of Europe*, vol. 1, book 2, p. 665. There were, for example, 3,000 students at Ashikaga in 1547. (See Boxer, *Christian Century*, p. 44.) Neither Oxford nor Cambridge achieved that size until the twentieth century.
29. Boxer, *Christian Century*, p. 29.
30. Fréderic, *Daily Life*, p. 231.
31. George B. Sansom, *The Western World and Japan*, p. 174.
32. Murdoch, *History of Japan*, II, p. 481.
33. Walter Dening, *The Life of Toyotomi Hideyoshi*, p. 74.
34. Charles Oman, *History of the Art of Warfare in the XVI Century*, p. 225.
35. Colonel Ernest M. Lloyd, *A Review of the History of Infantry*, p. 105. He is quoting Humphrey Barwick's 1594 estimate: ten arrows per minute for a good archer, forty shots per hour for a small arquebus or matchlock, twenty-five per hour for a large one or musket. Richard W. Barber in *The Knight and Chivalry*, p. 196, puts the rate of archery fire at twelve arrows per minute, which would make the disparity even greater.
36. John U. Nef, *War and Human Progress*, p. 32.
37. Donald Keene, ed. and tr., *Four Major Plays of Chikamatsu*, p. 71.
38. James W. Thompson, *The Wars of Religion in France, 1559–1576*, p. 383.
39. Kenneth Dean Butler, 'The *Heike Monogatari* and the Japanese Warrior Ethic,' p. 105.
40. Letter to the author from Professor Kiyondo Sato, who is

drawing on *Koyo Gunkan* and other sources.

41. Colonel Arcadi Gluckman, *United States Rifles, Muskets, and Carbines*, p. 28.

42. Brown, 'Impact of Firearms,' p. 239.

43. Yuzo Yamane, *Momoyama Genre Painting*, p. 155.

44. Sadler, *Maker of Modern Japan*, p. 105. Useful accounts of Nagashino are given in Sadler, pp. 100–105; in Turnbull, *Samurai*, pp. 156–160; in Michael Gibson, *The Samurai of Japan*, p. 53; and in George B. Sansom, *A History of Japan, 1334–1615*, pp. 287–288. The best map is in Turnbull.

45. Arima, *Kaho no Kigen to Sono Denryu*, p. 664. By the year of his death, 1582, Lord Oda had established cannon foundries on a large enough scale so that he was busy melting down temple bells to provide enough bronze. (Sansom, *A History of Japan, 1334–1615*, p. 309.)

46. Small cannon, however, the Japanese made superbly. A Western metallurgist who was in Japan in 1874 analyzed four kinds of bronze used to make cannon in the early seventeenth century. 'These old guns were admirably cast, and shew the cleverness of the Japanese in being able to found such large pieces of metal without the aid of western machinery,' reported A. J. C. Geerts in 'Useful Minerals and Metallurgy of the Japanese,' p. 48. Dr. Geerts added that these old guns were already scarce in 1874. In the preceding decade, European scrap dealers had bought them up by the hundred and shipped them home to be melted down. Some of the bronze may have wound up in belfries, in which case the cycle was complete: from temple bell to cannon to church bell.

47. T. C. Smout, *A History of the Scottish People, 1560–1830*, p. 103.

48. John Hill Burton, *History of Scotland*, V, 293–294.

49. Oman, *History of Art of Warfare*, p. 474. See also H. M. Baird, *The Huguenots and Henry of Navarre*, pp. 429–436, and Philippe Erlanger, *La Monarchie Française, 1515–1715*, vol. III, *Les Guerres de Religion*, pp. 174f. The Protestants, who were chanting Psalm 118 as they fired, credited the victory mainly to God, but it was an 'arquebusade' that killed Joyeuse's younger brother, and a pistol shot that killed the duke himself. (Erlanger, *La Monarchie*, III, p. 174.)

50. Nef, *War and Human Progress*, p. 91.

51. Stone, *Glossary of Arms*, p. 61. Japanese armor looks peculiar to Western eyes, but it was convenient for the wearer. 'A complete suit weighed only 25 pounds, and its wearer could run and jump in it with ease.' (Gibson, *Samurai*, p. 29.)

52. Sakakibara Kozan, *The Manufacture of Armour and Helmets in 16th-Century Japan*, p. 76. The story also appears in Stone, *Glossary*, p. 472.

53. The entire English army, for example, had fewer guns than any one of half a dozen Japanese feudal lords. Accurate figures for England are almost as hard to find as accurate figures for Japan – simply because guns and all other weapons were stockpiled by an enormous variety of local authorities, individual gentlemen, and even clergy, as well as by Her Majesty's Government; and there was no central tabulating agency. Furthermore, the army itself was neither a standing army, nor a series of feudal levies (as in Japan), but a cross between feudal levies and a sort of county draft, again without many central records.

   But some figures are available. For example, in 1569 the Privy Council of England had general musters held all over England to determine the number of soldiers

and weapons available in the event of invasion. The
Council naturally did not release the results. But the
French ambassador learned them through a spy, and reported back to Paris that 'the confidential number of soldiers arrived at' was 24,000, of whom about 6,000 had
guns. (Lindsay Boynton, *The Elizabethan Militia, 1558–
1638*, pp. 62–63.)

England was rapidly converting from the longbow to
the gun when the musters were held, and the number of
matchlocks grew very fast between 1569 and 1600. But
the number in Japan grew even faster. (Japan was, of
course, six times as populous a country.) Here is one
comparison. In 1589, Queen Elizabeth sent an army to
France to help Henry of Navarre secure the French
throne. It consisted of 3,600 men in four regiments, commanded by Lord Willoughby. Ideally (according to the
Privy Council), a regiment would have 60 percent gunners, 30 percent pikemen, and 10 percent halberdiers.
Realistically, it asked the London, Kent, Sussex, and
Hampshire regiments to come equipped 30 percent with
guns, 60 percent with pikes, and 10 percent with halberds. (G. C. Cruickshank, *Elizabeth's Army*, pp. 114,
237, 244.)

When the regiments actually assembled, almost all
were short of guns. The Hampshire regiment had a total
of twenty-six – not quite 3 percent. The armory in the
Tower of London was able to make up the deficit by issuing 300 extra guns – but that still meant the little
army sailed for France with something under 1,100 firearms. (Ibid., 243, 244.)

Five years earlier, in Japan, Lord Ryuzoji Takanobu,
who ruled not quite one of Japan's sixty-eight provinces,
arrived at a battle with 25,000 men, about 9,000 of them

gunners – 'with arquebuses so large they might almost be called muskets.' (Murdoch, *History of Japan*, II, 220.) Even allowing for the difference in population, it seems clear who was ahead in the manufacture of firearms.

54. Dening, *Toyotomi Hideyoshi*, p. 177. Other versions of the story do not mention the bow, but merely say he fought with a spear until his left arm was shattered by a bullet, at which point he retreated into his burning palace, where he either killed himself or perished in the flames. (See Turnbull, *Samurai*, pp. 163–164; Murdoch, *History of Japan*, II, pp. 176–178.)

55. Dening, *Toyotomi Hideyoshi*, p. 206; see also Turnbull, *Samurai*, p. 171.

56. And definitely waved his war fan. See the account of the Battle of Nagakute in Turnbull, *Samurai*, p. 176.

57. Murdoch, *History of Japan*, II, 369.

58. This plan 'did not appear fanciful or unrealistic to [Hideyoshi's] contemporaries.' On the contrary, they took it for granted that he *would* conquer China. Well before the invasion, some of the Japanese feudal lords were discussing which Chinese provinces to add to their domains; and a letter survives in which one of them is formally addressed as Lord of Taishu (in Chekiang Province, China). Similarly, Hideyoshi had invited the emperor to move permanently to China, leaving a cadet branch of the family behind in Kyoto, and the emperor had accepted. (Giuliana Stramigioli, 'Hideyoshi's Expansionist Policy on the Asiatic Mainland,' p. 100.)

59. For the Shimazu contingent, see Lach, *Asia on the Eve*, p. 149. Figures for the Tachibana contingent were supplied by Professor Kiyondo Sato, drawing on *Nihonsaikyoshi* and other sources.

60. J. L. Boots, 'Korean Weapons and Armour,' p. 24. Stcne believes that the Chinese weapons on which the Koreans had modeled theirs were the worst made in the sixteenth-century world. They still didn't have sights. (Stone, *Glossary of Arms*, p. 265.)

61. Ibid., p. 25. One should allow, of course, for some hyperbole in the Korean account. Matchlocks do not have rifled barrels, and are not usually that accurate. When Sir Henry Radecliff inspected the hundred men of the garrison in Portsmouth, England, in 1571, he found that twenty-three of them had matchlocks in working order. They had to shoot for him, and 'not fyve of them shott within fyve foote of a marke being sett within foure score yardes of them.' (Boynton, *Elizabethan Militia*, p. 113). Japanese marksmen with heavy-gauge weapons could doubtless do better than that – but rather seldom the hole of a coin at 500 feet.

62. Brown, 'Impact of Firearms,' p. 239.

63. Carletti, *My Voyage*, p. 112. The willingness of the samurai to use guns for hunting but not in battle exactly parallels the willingness of medieval European knights to use bows in hunting, though not in battle. (See A. T. Hatto, 'Archery and Chivalry: A Noble Prejudice,' pp. 41, 45.) Both are examples of what Hatto calls 'the stigma which attaches to missile weapons as a class.'

   The hero of Bertrand de Bar-sur-Aube's thirteenth-century poem *Le Roman de Girard de Viane* reveals the source of the stigma when he says, 'Cursed be the first man who became an archer; he was afraid and did not dare approach.' (Barber, *The Knight and Chivalry*, p. 196.)

64. Brown, 'Impact of Firearms,' p. 241. Cannon were in de-

mand, too. One general wrote home in 1593, 'Not long ago I dispatched two messengers to consult with you regarding cannon, [and again I insist] that you send me more. It does not matter what size they are. Inquire around the province, and send as many as can be found.' (Brown, 'Impact of Firearms,' p. 244.) They were needed for attacking Korean castles.

65. Nef, *War and Human Progress*, p. 137.
66. In a posthumous volume of *Table-Talk* – published the same year that Takeda Shingen, halfway around the world, was hailing the gun as the weapon of the future. (H. L. Mencken, *A New Dictionary of Quotations* (New York: Alfred A. Knopf, Inc., 1942), p. 140.)
67. Mikiso Hane, *Japan: A Historical Survey*, p. 166.
68. Letter to the author from Professor Lawrence Stone, History Department, Princeton.
69. Antonio de Morga, *Sucesos de las Islas Filipinas*, p. 318.
70. *History of the Empire of Japan*, p. 307. The Japanese leader was the famous Yamada Nagamasa (1585–1637), son of a kitchenware dealer in Suruga, who became Regent of Siam. There is a good account of him in Tadashige Matsumoto's *Stories of Fifty Japanese Heroes*, (Tokyo: Koseikaku, 1929).
71. Ryusaku Tsunoda, trans., *Japan in the Chinese Dynastic Histories*, p. 143.
72. John Whitney Hall, *Japan From Prehistory to Modern Times*, p. 180.
73. For early sword classifiers, see Alfred Dobree, *Japanese Sword Blades*, p. 9.
    For current ones, see Junji Homma, 'A History of Japanese "Old Swords," ' p. 253.
74. Hakusui, *Nippon-To*, p. xvii.

75. Ruth Benedict, *The Chrysanthemum and the Sword*, p. 296.

76. Sadler, *Maker of Modern Japan*, pp. 106, 80. The young man received the sword from Tokugawa Ieyasu – who had himself been given it five years earlier under identical circumstances, that is, after a battle in which *he* had used a matchlock.

77. Arima, *Kaho no Kigen to Sono Denryu*, p. 667. This isn't to say there was *no* ceremonial use of guns. There was. For example, in making an exchange of presents with one of the Hojo family in 1596, Ieyasu sent two famous swords plus a damascened gun of 'western barbarian' iron as his present. (Sadler, *Maker of Modern Japan*, p. 142.) For a time such presents were fairly common.

78. Nef, *War and Human Progress*, p. 129.

79. Ibid., p. 245.

80. Boxer, *Christian Century*, p. 245.

81. Japanese Ms. 53, 'Inatomi-ryu Teppo Densho,' Spencer Collection, New York Public Library.

82. The Inatomi were also famous gun manufacturers. There is a surviving story that says Lord Tokugawa Ieyasu was once out hunting cranes, and saw a specially fine one about 120 yards away. 'An ordinary gun won't carry,' he is supposed to have said, and had a special one made by Inatomi Gaiki brought. He got his crane. (Sadler, *Maker of Modern Japan*, p. 348.)

83. See Gibson, *Samurai*, p. 52; Sansom, *Japan: A Short Cultural History*, p. 433n; Sadler, *Maker of Modern Japan*, p. 229.

84. Arima, *Kaho no Kigen to Sono Denryu*, p. 657.

85. Ibid., p. 669.

86. John U. Nef, *Industry and Government in France and England, 1540–1640*, p. 61.

87. *Statutes of the Realm*, III, 215.

88. Paul L. Hughes and James F. Larkin, eds., *Tudor Royal Proclamations*, I, 177–179.
89. *Statutes of the Realm*, III, 457.
90. Ibid., III, 132.
91. *Tudor Royal Proclamations*, III, 261.
92. Arima, *Kaho no Kigen to Sono Denryu*, p. 670.
93. Junji Homma, *The Japanese Sword*, p. 58.
94. Ibid., p. 207.
95. Arima, *Kaho no Kigen to Sono Denryu*, p. 671.
96. Ibid., pp. 676–677.
97. The minor role that firearms came to play is reflected in the great eighteenth-century Japanese encyclopedia of weapons, *Honcho Gunkiko*. This twelve-volume work by the historian Arai Hakuseki was published in 1737. One volume is devoted to firearms. But as D. B. Waterhouse points out, there is 'no sign that he regarded them as more than curiosities.' ('Fire-arms in Japanese History; With Notes on a Japanese Wall Gun,' p. 95.)

    'He does not reveal much practical experience,' Waterhouse continues, 'for he says at one point, "the red barbarians' cannon . . . reaches with iron balls over 20 ri [nearly 49 miles]. It must be an exceedingly wonderful thing." ' (Waterhouse, 'Fire-arms,' p. 98. The 'red barbarians' are the Dutch, as opposed to the southern barbarians, or Portuguese and Spanish.)

    When two supplementary volumes of illustrations were published in 1740, they included no pictures of firearms at all.
98. Pratt, *History of Japan*, pp. 243–244, 265.
99. Arima, *Kaho no Kigen to Sono Denryu*, pp. 659–661.
100. Ibid. p. 677.
101. Yosaburo Takekoshi, *Economic Aspects of the History of Japan*, 95.

102. Cary, *Christianity in Japan*, I, p. 227.
103. Yoshi S. Kuno, *Japanese Expansion on the Asiatic Continent*, II, p. 340.
104. Robert E. Kimbrough, 'Japanese Firearms,' pp. 464–465.
105. François Caron and Joost Schouten, *A True Description of the Mighty Kingdoms of Japan and Siam*, p. xxxiv.
106. Boxer, *Christian Century*, p. 285.
107. Montanus, *Atlas Japannensis*, p. 352.
108. Boxer, *Jan Compagnie in Japan*, p. 113.
109. Charles Peter Thunberg, *Travels in Europe, Africa, and Asia*, III, 51.
110. M. M. Busk (originally published anonymously), *Manners and Customs of the Japanese . . . From Recent Dutch Visitors of Japan*, pp. 415–416.
111. J. E. Kidder, *Japan Before Buddhism*, p. 57.
112. Pollard, *History of Firearms*, p. 37.
113. V. M. Golovnin, *Memoirs of a Captivity in Japan During the Years 1811, 1812, and 1813*, I, 113.
114. Ibid., II, 330.
115. Ibid., III, 229–230.
116. Robert S. Gallagher, 'Castaways on Forbidden Shores,' p. 34.
These stage-prop forts (designed, like Chinese firecrackers, to frighten enemies at a distance) were extremely common in mid-nineteenth-century Japan. Bayard Taylor, the American poet and novelist, who managed to join Perry's 1853 expedition as an acting master's mate, was fascinated by them, and also rather scornful. The Japanese unrolled a big one made of black canvas the first night the squadron was anchored off Japan. Taylor spent much of the next day examining it with binoculars. And then he notes, 'These diversions they repeated so often during our stay, that at last we ceased to

regard them; but it was amusing to hear some of our old quarter-masters now and then gravely report to Captain Buchanan: "Another dungaree fort thrown up, sir!" ' (Bayard Taylor, *A Visit to India, China, and Japan in the Year 1853*, p. 419.)

117. Allan B. Cole, ed., *With Perry in Japan: The Diary of Edward Yorke McCauley*, p. 117.

118. Ryusaku Tsunoda, et al., eds., *Sources of the Japanese Tradition*, p. 568.

119. Ibid., p. 615.

120. E. W. Clement, 'The Saga and Satsuma Rebellions,' pp. 23–24.

121. Ibid., p. 27.

122. Murdoch, *History of Japan*, II, 658.

123. A. C. Maclay, *A Budget of Letters From Japan*, p. 299.

124. F. J. Norman, *The Fighting Man of Japan*, p. 30. Norman, a former British cavalry officer, became the first Westerner since the seventeenth century fully to master Japanese swordsmanship. He began his study in 1868, under the fencing instructor of the last Tokugawa shogun. He claimed that 'the Japanese system of two-handed swordsmanship is much superior to any of the systems in Europe.' (Norman, *Fighting Man*, p. 42.)

125. James H. Buck, 'The Satsuma Rebellion of 1877,' p. 440.

126. Elizabeth T. Nock, ed., 'The Satsuma Rebellion of 1877: Letters of John Capen Hubbard,' pp. 371–372.

127. Bayard Taylor, *A History of Germany*, p. 295. See also Hajo Holborn, *A History of Modern Germany*. Holborn summarizes the quality of middle-European life in the mid-seventeenth century as follows: 'A barbarism from which death was the only release had settled over Germany.' (Vol. I, p. 354.) As for population, Holborn reports that in some German states, such as the Palatinate,

only a third of the population survived. In all the German states put together, the population dropped from about twenty million in 1618 to about twelve and a half million in 1648. (Vol. II, p. 22–23.)
128. Engelbert Kaempfer, *History of Japan*, III, p. 336.

POSTSCRIPT

1. Martine Legge, 'A Dormant Male Talent,' p. 12. See also John Beckman, *A History of Inventions and Discoveries*, IV, p. 317.
2. Arnold Toynbee, 'Our Tormenting Dilemma,' p. 8.
3. Rene Dubos, quoted in 'Bard College: The Slowing of Technology,' *The New York Times*, June 14, 1971, p. 44.
4. 'The popular Western view that the Tokugawa Period represents an unhappy period of stagnation between the first and second encounters with the West has now been erased from all but the world history textbooks.' (John Whitney Hall, *Japanese History: New Dimensions*, p. 37.)
5. *Japan, Its Land, People, and Culture*, pp. 334–335.
6. Hideomi Tuge, *Historical Development of Science and Technology in Japan*, p. 44.
7. Ibid., p. 50.
8. Ibid.
9. Ibid.
10. *Japan, Its Land, People, and Culture*, p. 463.
11. Reischauer, *The Japanese*, p. 171.
12. Albert Craig and Donald Shively, eds., *Personality in Japanese History*, pp. 134, 131.
13. Ibid., p. 145.
14. Hane, *Japan*, p. 235.

15. Craig and Shively, *Personality*, p. 149.
16. Tuge, *Science and Technology in Japan*, p. 74.
17. Ibid.
18. Golovnin, *Memoirs*, III, 202.
19. Edward S. Morse, *Japan Day by Day*, I, p. 23.
20. Ibid., p. 47.
21. Alfred Crofts and Percy Buchanan, *A History of the Far East*, p. 106.
22. Morse, *Japan Day by Day*, I, pp. 42–43.
23. Mario Cosenza, ed., *The Complete Journals of Townsend Harris*, p. 287.
24. 'We are living in the world's most polluted country.' Jun Ui, 'A Basic Theory of *Kogai*,' *Science and Society in Modern Japan*, ed. Nakayama Shigeru et al., p. 294. *Kogai* can be translated either broadly as 'public hazard' or narrowly as 'environmental pollution.'
25. Henry Heuskan, *Japan Journal, 1855–1861*, p. 151.
26. Mario Cosenza, ed., *Complete Journals of Townsend Harris*, pp. 440–441, 428–429.
27. Sir Rutherford Alcock, *The Capital of the Tycoon*, I, p. 383.
28. Edward Barrington de Fonblanque, *Niphon and Pe-che-li, or, Two Years in Japan and Northern China*, p. 68.
29. Ibid., p. 61.
30. Morse, *Japan Day by Day*, I, 44.

ACKNOWLEDGMENTS
& SOURCES

Since the author of this book does not read Japanese, he could not possibly have written it without the help of Eishoku Kuroda of the class of 1965 at Dartmouth, who translated for him Admiral Seiho Arima's book *Kaho no Kigen to Sono Denryu*. Still less could he have written it without the help of Kiyondo Sato, Professor of Aesthetics at Sacred Heart University, Tokyo, and descendent of the Lords Itakura (one of whom commanded at the siege of Shimabara in 1637). Dr. Sato translated a great many sixteenth-century Japanese documents – and not merely translated them, he interpreted them, made sense of them, put them into perspective. Least of all could he have written it without the free year provided him by the Guggenheim Foundation as one of its fellows. For that he owes thanks not only to the Foundation, but to Jonathan Mirsky, then Professor of Chinese at Dartmouth, and the late Ivan Morris, Professor of Japanese at Columbia, with whose assistance he got the fellowship. (This does not make either of them responsible for errors in the book.)

He is further indebted to Professor Lawrence Stone of the history department at Princeton for information on the number of English gentry in 1600; to the late Sir George Sansom for information on Hideyoshi's sword hunt (actually, sword-and-gun hunt) in 1587; to Robert T. Singer of Kyoto for extraordinary help in finding illustrations, and for much good advice; to Dr. Yoshiuke Nakano of Enfield, New Hampshire, for help in interpreting inscriptions; and to Professor John Major of the Dartmouth history department for instruction on the whole relevant span of Japanese and Korean history. John Major pointed out many errors that I corrected, and a few that I have chosen to leave – such as that while the samurai did indeed rely on swords as their principal ornamentation, to the complete exclusion of jewelry, they also possessed *mon* or crests, and they sometimes had the family *mon* embroidered on their clothing. My excuse is the desire to keep the narrative as simple as a complex subject will permit – and especially to keep learned detail to a manageable proportion.

Here is the reason. While I naturally hope that professional students of Japan will read this book (and with an indulgent eye, at that), they are not the primary audience. The primary audience is the much larger group of people interested in the possibility of controlling technology. To them the fact that the story takes place in Japan will be incidental, and for them a mass of precise detail about Japanese feudal life would be out of place. It is for their sake, for example, that I have mainly used the familiar term 'samurai,' even though I am well aware that *bushi* is the inclusive and more correct term for the military class in feudal Japan. And that I have in every case but one called the great city on the Kanto plain 'Tokyo,' even though its name was 'Edo' until the Meiji emperor moved there in 1868. And that I have omitted the guides to pronunciation known as macrons. Properly speaking, I should have written *teppō, daimyō*, and *Chōshu*—but to my eye that merely makes the text harder to read.

Anyone wishing to follow the author through his reading in

source material would have to read seven or eight hundred books and articles, a surprising number of them almost worthless. (Histories of Korea, for some reason, are preeminent in worthlessness. I read all I could find – and the best of them was little above the missionary memoir or government propaganda level.) I shall here list only about a hundred and twenty sources: all the works – except common reference books – from which I have directly drawn, and a few other books and articles which I found particularly useful as background. References to *TASJ* are to the *Transactions of the Asiatic Society of Japan*.

All the works listed except two are in English. Students of Japanese history will know well enough where to find *Teppo-ki*, or that eyewitness account of Lord Hideyoshi's invasion of Korea called *Chosen Monogatari*. A broader group of scholars could read Dr. A. Pfizmaier's two-volume translation of *Chosen Monogatari*, published in 1875 as *Der Feldzug der Japaner Gegen Corea im Yahre 1597*. Most of us need books in English.

Even in English there is no attempt to include all works of value. For example, Charles Boxer is represented by two books and one article. He has written a dozen other books and articles that throw at least a gleam of light on Japanese military history or on Japanese control of technology, and I have read them with profit. But what I mean to offer is a small central list. For the convenience of the reader, I have divided this list into two parts: first books on Japan, and then all others.

BIBLIOGRAPHY

JAPAN

Alcock, Sir Rutherford. *The Capital of the Tycoon.* 2 vols. New York: Harper and Brothers, 1863.

Arima, Seiho. *Kaho no Kigen to Sono Denryu (The Origin of Firearms and Their Early Transmission).* Tokyo: Yoshi-kawa Kobunkan, 1962.

Benedict, Ruth. *The Chrysanthemum and the Sword.* Boston: Houghton Mifflin Company, 1946.

Bolitho, Harold. *Treasures Among Men: The Fudai Daimyo in Tokugawa Japan.* New Haven, Conn.: Yale University Press, 1974.

Boxer, Charles R. *The Christian Century in Japan.* Berkeley: University of California Press, 1951.

———. *Jan Compagnie in Japan*, rev. ed. The Hague: Nijhoff, 1950.

———. 'Notes on Early European Military Influence in Japan.' *TASJ*, 2nd series, vol. 8 (1931), pp. 67–93.

Brinkley, Frank. *A History of the Japanese People.* New York: Encyclopaedia Britannica Co., 1915.

Brown, Delmer M. 'The Impact of Firearms on Japanese Warfare.' *Far Eastern Quarterly* now the *Journal of Asian Studies*, vol. 7 (1947/48), pp. 236–253.

Buck, James. 'The Satsuma Rebellion of 1877.' *Monumenta Nipponica*, vol. 28 (1973), pp. 427–446.

Busk, M.M. (originally published anonymously). *Manners and Customs of the Japanese*. London: J. Murray, 1841.

Butler, Kenneth D. 'The *Heike Monogatari* and the Japanese Warrior Ethic.' *Harvard Journal of Asiatic Studies*, vol. 29 (1969), pp. 93–108.

Carletti, Francesco. *My Voyage Around the World*, tr. Herbert Weinstock. New York: Pantheon, 1964.

Caron, François, and Schouten Joost. *A True Description of the Mighty Kingdoms of Japan and Siam*, ed. Charles R. Boxer. London: Argonaut Press, 1935.

Cary, Otis. *A History of Christianity in Japan*. 2 vols. New York: F. H. Revell, 1909.

Clement, E. W. 'The Saga and Satsuma Rebellions.' *TASJ*, vol. 50 (1922).

Cole, Allan B., ed. *With Perry in Japan: The Diary of Edward Yorke McCauley*. Princeton, N.J.: Princeton University Press, 1942.

———, ed. *Yankee Surveyors in the Shogun's Seas*. Princeton, N.J.: Princeton University Press, 1947.

Coleridge, Henry James. *The Life and Letters of St. Francis Xavier*. 2 vols. London: Burns and Oates, 1890.

Cooper, Michael. *Rodrigues the Interpreter*. New York: Weatherhill, 1974.

———, ed. *The Southern Barbarians*, Tokyo: Kodansha, 1971.

Cosenza, Mario, ed. *The Complete Journal of Townsend Harris*. N.Y.: Japan Society, 1930.

Craig, Albert, and Shively, Donald, eds. *Personality in Japanese History*. Berkeley: University of California Press, 1970.

Crofts, Alfred, and Buchanan, Percy. *A History of the Far East.* New York: Longmans, Green, 1958.

De Fonblanque, Edward Barrington. *Niphon and Pe-che-li; or Two Years in Japan and Northern China.* London: Saunders, Otley, 1862.

Dening, Walter. *The Life of Toyotomi Hideyoshi,* 3rd ed. Kobe and London: J. L. Thompson, 1930.

Dobree, Alfred. *Japanese Sword Blades.* York, Pa.: G. Shumway, 1971. (Original publication 1905).

Draeger, Donn, and Smith, Robert W. *Asian Fighting Arts.* New York: Berkeley, 1974.

Duus, Peter. *Feudalism in Japan.* N.Y.: Alfred A. Knopf, 1969.

Gallagher, Robert. 'Castaways on Forbidden Shores.' *American Heritage,* vol. 19, no. 4 (June 1968), pp. 34–37.

Geerts, A. J. C. 'Useful Minerals and Metallurgy of the Japanese.' *TASJ,* vol. 3, pt. 1 (1874), pp. 1–16, 27–51, 85–97.

Gibson, Michael. *The Samurai of Japan.* London: Wayland, 1973.

Glamann, K. 'The Dutch East India Company's Trade in Japanese Copper.' *Scandinavian Economic History Review,* vol. 2 (1953), pp. 41–103.

Golovnin, V.M. *Memoirs of a Captivity in Japan During the Years 1811, 1812, and 1813.* 3 vols. London: H. Colburn, 1824.

Hakusui, Inami. *Nippon-To, the Japanese Sword.* Tokyo: Cosmo, 1948.

Hall, John Whitney. *Japan From Prehistory to Modern Times.* New York: Delacorte Press, 1970.

―――. *Japanese History: New Dimensions.* Washington: American Historical Association, 1961.

Hane, Mikiso. *Japan: A Historical Survey.* New York: Charles Scribner's Sons, 1972.

Heusken, Henry. *Japan Journal, 1855–1861*, tr. J. C. van der Corput and Wilson, R. A. New Brunswick, N.J.: Rutgers University Press, 1964.

Hickman, Money, and Fetchko, Peter. *Japan Day by Day: An Exhibition Honoring Edward Sylvester Morse*. Salem: Peabody Museum, 1977.

History of the Empire of Japan, by the Committee for Historiographical Compilation in the Imperial University, tr. F. Brinkley. Tokyo: Dai Nippon Tosho Kabushiki Kwaisha, 1893.

Homma, Junji. 'A History of Japanese "Old Swords." ' *Japan Science Review: Literature, Philosophy and History*, vol. 4 (1953), pp. 253–257.

———. *The Japanese Sword*. Tokyo: Kogei-sha, 1948.

Japan, Its Land, People, and Culture, compiled by the Japanese National Commission for UNESCO, rev. ed. Tokyo: Ministry of Finance, 1964.

Kaempfer, Engelbert. *History of Japan*. 3 vols. Glasgow: J. MacLehose, 1906.

Keene, Donald. *The Japanese Discovery of Europe*. New York: Grove Press, 1954.

———. *Four Major Plays of Chikamatsu*. New York: Columbia University Press, 1961.

Kidder, J. E. *Japan Before Buddhism*. New York: Praeger, 1959.

Kimbrough, Robert E. 'Japanese Firearms.' *The Gun Collector*, no. 33 (1950), pp. 445–465.

Kozan, Sakakibara. *The Manufacture of Armour and Helmets in Sixteenth-Century Japan*, rev. and ed. H. Russell Robinson. London: Holland Press, 1962.

Kuno, Yoshi S. *Japanese Expansion on the Asiatic Continent*. 2 vols. Berkeley: University of California Press, 1940.

Lach, Donald F. *Asia in the Making of Europe*. 2 vols. Chicago:

University of Chicago Press 1965–70.

————. ed., *Asia on the Eve of Europe's Expansion*. Englewood Cliffs, N.J.: Prentice-Hall, 1965.

Louis-Frédéric (pseud.). *Daily Life in Japan at the Time of the Samurai*. London: G. Allen, 1972.

Maclay, A.C. *A Budget of Letters From Japan*. 2nd ed. New York: A. C. Armstrong, 1889.

Montanus, Arnoldus. *Atlas Japannensis*, English'd by John Ogilby, Esq. London: T. Johnson, 1670.

Morse, Edward S. *Japan Day by Day*. 2 vols. Boston: Houghton Mifflin Company, 1917.

Murdoch, James. *A History of Japan*. 3 vols. London: K. Paul, Trench, Trubner, 1925.

Nock, Elizabeth T., ed. 'The Satsuma Rebellion of 1877: Letters of John Capen Hubbard.' *Far Eastern Quarterly*, vol. 7 (1947/48), pp. 368–375.

Norman, F. J. *The Fighting Man of Japan*. London: Constable, 1905.

Pratt, Peter. *History of Japan, Compiled From Records of the English East India Company*, ed. M. B. T. Paske-Smith. Kobe: J. L. Thompson, 1931.

Reischauer, Edwin O. *The Japanese*. Cambridge, Mass.: Harvard University Press, 1977.

Riess, Ludwig. 'History of the English Factory at Hirado.' *TASJ*, vol. 26 (1898), pp. 1–115, 163–218.

Robinson, Basil W. *Arms and Armour of Old Japan*. London: H. M. Stationery Office, 1951.

Rodrigues, Joao. *This Island of Japon*, tr. and ed. Michael Cooper. Tokyo: Kodansha, 1973.

Sadler, A. L. *The Maker of Modern Japan: The Life of Tokugawa Ieyasu*. London: G. Allen and Unwin, 1937.

Sansom, George B. *A History of Japan to 1867*. 3 vols. Stanford:

Stanford University Press, 1958–63.

———. *Japan: A Short Cultural History*, rev. ed. New York: Appleton-Century-Crofts, 1962.

———. *The Western World and Japan*. New York: Alfred A. Knopf, 1950.

Shigeru, Nakayama, et al., eds. *Science and Society in Modern Japan*. Cambridge, Mass.: MIT Press, 1974.

Stone, George Cameron. *A Glossary of the Construction, Decoration, and Use of Arms and Armor*. Portland, Me.: Southworth Press, 1934.

Stramigioli, Giuliana. 'Hideyoshi's Expansionist Policy on the Asiatic Mainland.' *TASJ*, 3rd series, vol. 3 (1954), pp. 74–116.

Takekoshi, Yosaburo. *The Economic Aspects of the History of the Civilization Japan*. 3 vols. New York: Macmillan Company, 1930.

Taylor, Bayard. *A Visit to India, China, and Japan in the Year 1853*. New York: G. P. Putnam, 1867.

Temple, Sir Richard, ed. *The Travels of Peter Mundy*, vol. III, pt. I. Cambridge, England: Hakluyt Society, 1919 (Second Series, vol. 45).

Thunberg, Charles Peter. *Travels in Europe, Africa, and Asia*, vol. 3. London: F. and C. Rivington, 1795.

Tsunoda, Ryusaku. *Japan in the Chinese Dynastic Histories*. South Pasadena, Calif.: P. D. and Ione Perkins, 1951.

——— et al., eds. *Sources of the Japanese Tradition*. New York: Columbia University Press, 1958.

Tuge, Hideomi, ed. *Historical Development of Science and Technology in Japan*, rev. ed. Tokyo: *Kokusai Bunka Shinkokai*, 1968.

Turk, F. A. *The Prints of Japan*. New York: October House, 1966.

Turnbull, S. R. *The Samurai: A Military History*. New York: Macmillan Company, 1977.

Varley, H. Paul. *Samurai*. New York: Delacorte Press, 1971.

Waterhouse, D. B. 'Fire-arms in Japanese History: With Notes on a Japanese Wall Gun.' *British Museum Quarterly*, vol. 27 (1963/64), pp. 94–99.

Yamane, Yuzo. *Momoyama Genre Painting*, tr. John Shields. New York.: Weatherhill, 1973.

Yumoto, John M. *The Samurai Sword*. Rutland, Vt.: C. E. Tuttle, 1958.

OUTSIDE JAPAN

Ayalon, David. *Gunpowder and Firearms in the Mamluk Kingdom: A Challenge to a Medieval Society*. London: Vallentine, Mitchell, 1956.

Baird, H. M. *The Huguenots and Henry of Navarre*. New York: Charles Scribner's Sons, 1886.

Barber, Richard W., *The Knight and Chivalry*. New York: Charles Scribner's Sons, 1970.

Beckmann, John. *A History of Inventions and Discoveries*, tr. and rev. by William Johnston. 4 vols. London: J. Walker, 1814.

Boots, J. L. 'Korean Weapons and Armour.' *Transactions of the Korea Branch of the Royal Asiatic Society*, vol. 23, pt. 2 (1934), pp. 1–37.

Boynton, Lindsay. *The Elizabethan Militia, 1558–1638*. London: Routledge and Kegan Paul, 1967.

Burton, John Hill. *History of Scotland*, vol. 5. Edinburgh: W. Blackwood, 1898.

Cipolla, Carlo. *Guns and Sails in the Early Phase of European*

Expansion, 1400–1700. London: Collins, 1965.

Cruickshank, C. G. *Army Royal.* Oxford: Oxford University Press, 1969.

————. *Elizabeth's Army.* 2nd ed. (rev.). Oxford: Oxford University Press, 1966.

Erlanger, Philippe. *La Monarchie Francaise, 1515–1715,* vol. 3. Paris: J. Tallandier, 1971.

Gluckman, Arcadi. *United States Muskets, Rifles, and Carbines.* Buffalo, N.Y.: O. Ulbrich, 1948.

Goodman, Grant K. *The Dutch Impact on Korea, 1640–1853.* Leiden: E. J. Brill, 1967.

Hatto, A. T. 'Archery and Chivalry: A Noble Prejudice.' *Modern Language Review,* vol. 35 (1940), pp. 40–54.

Hayward, John F. *The Art of the Gunmaker,* vol. I, 1500–1660. New York: St. Martin's Press, 1962.

Hogden, Margaret T. *Change and History: A Study of the Dated Distribution of Technological Innovations in England,* Viking Fund Publications in Anthropology no. 18. New York: Wenner-Gren Foundation, 1952.

Holborn, Hajo. *A History of Modern Germany.* 3 vols. New York: Alfred A. Knopf 1970/71.

Hughes, Paul L., and Larkin, James F. *Tudor Royal Proclamations.* 3 vols. New Haven, Conn.: Yale University Press, 1964–69.

Jeon, Sang-woon. *Science and Technology in Korea.* Cambridge, Mass.: MIT Press, 1974.

Ledyard, Gari. *The Dutch Come to Korea.* Seoul: Royal Asiatic Society, 1971.

Legge, Martine. 'A Dormant Male Talent.' *The Observer* (London), February 19, 1961, p. 12.

Lenk, Torsten. *The Flintlock, Its Origin and Development,* rev. ed. London: Holland Press, 1965.

Lloyd, Ernest M. *A Review of the History of Infantry*. London: Longmans, 1908.

Merton, Robert K. *Science, Technology, and Society in Seventeenth- Century England*. New York: H. Fertig, 1970.

Morga, Antonio de. *Sucesos de las Islas Filipinas*, ed. and tr. J. S. Cummins. Cambridge, England: Cambridge University Press for the Hayluyt Society, 1971.

Nambo, Heizo, 'Who Invented the Explosives?' *Japanese Studies in the History of Science*, vol. 9 (1970), pp. 49–98.

Nef, John U. *The Conquest of the Material World*. Chicago: University of Chicago Press, 1964.

———. *Industry and Government in France and England, 1540–1640*. Philadelphia: American Philosophical Society, 1940.

———. *War and Human Progress*. Cambridge, Mass.: Harvard University Press, 1950.

Oman, Sir Charles. *History of the Art of Warfare in the XVI Century*. London: Methuen, 1937.

Pollard, Hugh B. C. *A History of Firearms*. Boston: Houghton, Mifflin Company, 1936.

Silver, George. *Paradoxes of Defence* ('Wherein is proved the true grounds of Fight to be in the short auncient weapons'). London: Edward Blount, 1599.

Smout, T. C. *A History of the Scottish People, 1560–1830*, New York: Charles Scribner's Sons, 1969.

Taylor, Bayard. *A History of Germany*, ed. and rev. Professor Sidney B. Fay. New York: P. F. Collier, 1928.

Thompson, James W. *The Wars of Religion in France, 1559–1576*. Chicago: University of Chicago Press, 1909.

Toynbee, Arnold. 'Our Tormenting Dilemma.' *The Observer* (London), August 10, 1958.

Wilbur, C. Martin. 'The History of the Crossbow.' *The Smithsonian Report for 1936*, pp. 427–438.

Noel Perrin

Finally, there is one book to mention which is not source material for this study, and which is not even concerned with the real world. But anyone who has been interested enough to come this far and who doesn't yet know *Islandia* clearly should read it.

Islandia is a novel that imagines the other road, the one that the Japanese weren't able to take after 1854. Islandia, like Tokugawa Japan, is a country closed to foreigners and to industrial revolutions. It is highly civilized, traditional, and agricultural; it has about three million people. It also has one factory, making quite modern guns.

In October 1904, under heavy pressure from the great powers, Islandia considers opening its copper mines, coal beds, and other resources to rapid Western development. Lord Mora, the prime minister, signs a treaty with the Germans that is, in the book's words, 'somewhat similar to that of Perry and the Japanese.' As in Japan, railroads are to be built, concessions developed, the whole life changed. In the end, the Islandians decide that these are gifts they don't want. Unlike the Japanese in 1854, they succeed in expelling the foreigners again. They resume living in steady state, utilizing technology with great selectivity.

Some people, myself included, think *Islandia* is the best utopian novel ever written. It is, in any case, the one most germane to the question of the control of technology.

Wright, Austin Tappan. *Islandia*. New York: Farrar and Rinehart, 1942.

Giving Up the Gun
was designed by Richard Hendel,
typeset by G & S Typesetters, Inc.,
and composed in Intertype Waverley, a face
based upon the designs of Justus Erich Walbaum,
a typefounder active in Germany in the early nineteenth
century. Waverley is close in spirit to the refined and attenuated
types first introduced by Firmin Didot, designs that accentuated the thicks
and the thins, carried the stress along a horizontal rather than a diagonal
axis, and were cut along fairly strict geometrical principles. Waverley
is more subtle than these French faces, its contours softened by
the sensitivity of the handcraftsman who cut it, and its
sharp angularities modified by the influence of Pierre
Simon Fournier's transitional designs. The book
was printed by Malloy Lithographing, Inc.